Boys and Girls

BOYS & GIRLS

Superheroes in the Doll Corner

Vivian Gussin Paley

With a Foreword by Philip W. Jackson

THE UNIVERSITY OF CHICAGO PRESS
Chicago and London

In memory of my father
Dr. Harry A. Gussin

The University of Chicago Press, Chicago 60637
The University of Chicago Press, Ltd., London
© 1984 by The University of Chicago
All rights reserved. Published 1984
Paperback edition 1986
Printed in the United States of America
09 08 07 06 05 04   8 9 10 11 12 13

Library of Congress Cataloging in Publication Data
Paley, Vivian Gussin, 1929–
    Boys & girls.

    1. Kindergarten—United States—Case studies.
2. Child development—Case studies.   3. Play—Case
studies.   4. Identity (Psychology)—Case studies.   6. Teaching—
Case studies.   I. Title.   II. Title: Boys and girls.
LB1195.P18   1984   372′.218′.0973   84-93
ISBN 0-226-64492-8 (paper)

Foreword

What are little boys made of? Why, snips and snails and puppy dogs' tails, of course. And little girls? What else but sugar and spice and everything nice? "*Everybody* knows *that*," the child within us wants to insist. Everybody, that is, who was brought up listening to the rhymes of Mother Goose, as I certainly was.

But what of the truth embedded in those well-remembered lines? Is there any there at all? "Absolutely not," today's voice of opinion informs. "As a matter of fact," it continues, "not only are those old rhymes totally false; they are potentially harmful. They serve to perpetuate a pair of stereotypes that we would do well to eliminate—those of the "nasty" boy and the "dainty" girl—neither of which has any basis in fact."

But is that so? Isn't there nearly always at least a grain of truth in stereotypes? How else can we account for their durability?

In this intriguing book, Vivian Paley confronts us with a portion of the truth that lies behind that particular pair of stereotypes. Reporting on the play patterns and fantasies of a group of kindergarteners with whom she worked as a teacher, Paley leads her readers to conclude that Mother Goose may not have been so far off the mark after all.

The little boys in Paley's class clearly have *something* in their background or in their makeup that makes them fidgety and rambunctious in a way the little girls in the class are not. The latter, in turn, though perhaps not as sugary sweet as Mother Goose makes them out to be, emerge as creatures strikingly different from their rough-and-tumble male class-mates.

Why this should be so is not a question that occupies Paley nearly so much as do the facts themselves and their significance for education. She is, after all, a teacher whose job it is to accept her pupils as she finds them, without becoming over-ly concerned about how or why they came to be as they are. The differences she observes between the boys and girls in her class are there whether she wants them to be or not. What Paley seeks, and what she offers her readers, is a heightened sensitivity to what children of kindergarten age are like and a greater appreciation of the differences to be found among them.

That accomplishment provides reason enough to recommend this book to anyone who wants to know more about young children. Readers who come to the book with that interest alone will surely not be disappointed. But *Boys and Girls* is more than an insightful book about kindergarteners and, indirectly, children in general. It is also a book about a kindergarten teacher and, even more indirectly, about teaching in general. What it has to say about the latter is, in my judgment, fully as informative and important, though by no means as explicit, as is its contribution to our understanding of children. Because the theme of teaching and what it is like to be a teacher is not so clearly drawn as it might have been (I suspect Paley's modesty accounts for that), a few words about that theme and its contribution to the book's value would seem to be in order.

The boys and girls in Paley's room changed noticeably between September and June, as young children are known to do. But so did their teacher. By the time spring rolled around, she was no longer the person she had been in the fall. She had started out with a rather low tolerance for the aggressiveness expressed in the fantasy play of the boys. She had also begun with a general feeling of acceptance toward the more "domesticated" play of the girls. By the end of the year, both of those attitudes had undergone a significant change. She wound up considerably more tolerant of the play patterns of the boys and rather less comfortable about certain aspects of what the girls were doing. In short, she ended the year a much more open-minded and, I would say, a wiser teacher than she was at the start. The hope is that all who read this book may similarly benefit.

Even more important than the specific changes Paley underwent during the course of the school year is what her account reveals about the preconditions of her growth as a teacher and, therefore, what it says about the desired attitudes and personal dispositions of teachers everywhere—and parents, too, for that matter! The lessons it contains on this topic may be as hoary as the Mother Goose rhyme the children's behavior calls to mind, but they are valuable all the same. Today's parents and teachers, no less than yesterday's, would do well to heed them.

The most important of these lessons has to do with a willingness to be self-critical in a searching, yet positive, way. Its most concise formulation is the ancient Socratic adage. Know thyself, with the "knowing" it speaks of taken to mean not just passive acceptance of the way one is, but a critical look at how one might become better. Within the context of classroom teaching, what this kind of knowing entails, at least as a first step, is a readiness to face up to one's own shortcomings as a teacher, even when it hurts to do so and when doing so means letting one's students know that a mistake has been made. It also requires a willingness to change, which means actively seeking new ways of doing things and consciously adopting new attitudes and new outlooks to replace the old. The fundamental requirement is, in a word, courage.

Vivian Paley is courageous. She excels in the capacity to look at herself as a teacher in an unflinching way. That she does so with more than a touch of humor makes the process all the more appealing to those of her readers who would dare to make the same sort of self examination. Reading of her occasional blunders as a teacher and of her efforts to correct them, all fully admitted and wholesomely confronted, we are encouraged to face up to weaknesses of our own and thereby to begin the often painful process of doing something about them.

That lesson alone, if taken to heart, would make a real difference in the lives of all who have not yet heeded its wisdom. The fact that it is but one of many such lessons to be culled from the pages to follow should make the prospect of reading them all the more inviting. The sheer enjoyment of doing so also awaits everyone who retains the capacity to be captivated by what young children say and do. In the best of all possible worlds, that would include us all.

Philip W. Jackson

Preface

Kindergarten is a triumph of sexual self-stereotyping. No amount of adult subterfuge or propaganda deflects the five-year-old's passion for segregation by sex. They think they have invented the differences between boys and girls and, as with any new invention, must prove that it works. The doll corner is often the best place to collect evidence. It is not simply a place to play; it is a stronghold against ambiguity.

When the children separate by sex, I, the teacher, am more often on the girls' side. We move at the same pace and reach for the same activities, while the boys barricade themselves in the blocks, periodically making forays into female territory.

Janie runs out of the doll corner shouting "I'm telling!" She finds me at the sink. "Me and Mary Ann and Charlotte and Karen were playing in there and they came in and started shooting!"

Mary Ann is at her side now and adds her own complaints: "They spoiled everything. Andrew was where we put the clothes and Jeremy was on top of the refrigerator and Paul stuck his fingers in my face."

The boys are still in the doll corner. "What were you playing, Andrew?" I ask.

"Cops and robbers."

"In the doll corner?"

"We need to steal food. And also gold. Because we're the bad guys. We're robbers."

"Well, you can't play that in the doll corner. Play it outside, later."

"Can't we do it in the blocks?"

"No. No shooting. That's only for outside."

An ordinary kindergarten confrontation has taken place, but our visitor, Charlotte's mother, is concerned. "They used to play so nicely in the doll corner," she says, "in nursery school, the boys and girls together. Now Charlotte tells me the boys are always fighting."

"It's mostly pretend," I say. "And, by the way, they didn't play all that nicely in nursery school."

"Maybe they should just stay out of the doll corner," the visitor suggests.

"If only they could."

The boys have been trying to leave the doll corner since they came to kindergarten. They are superheroes now—or feel they should be. The girls do not object to superheroes or robbers in the doll corner as long as they play the way girls play. Like Charlotte's mother, the girls remember when boys were more at ease in female surroundings.

Domestic play looks remarkably alike for both sexes at age three. Costumes representing male and female roles are casually exchanged. Everyone cooks and eats pretend food together. Mother, father, and baby are the primary actors, but identities shift and the participants seldom keep one another informed. Policemen sweep the floor and dress the baby, and mothers put men's vests over negligees while making vague appointments on the telephone. If asked, a boy will likely say he is the father, but if he were to say mother, it would cause little concern. It can be a peaceful place, this three-year-old's doll corner, even if monsters and superheroes enter, for the cooking and dressing and telephoning are usually private affairs.

By the age of four, the players are more inclined to tell one another who they are and what they are doing. They want to coordinate themes, but it is not always possible, because the boys are beginning to rebel. The girls prefer one mother, one father, and one baby per household and will play auxiliary parts when necessary: sisters, pets, grandmothers, teenagers, and baby-sitters. They would like the boys to be plumbers, carpenters, and firemen, but some boys would rather be monsters or superheroes.

The four-year-old boy is less comfortable in the doll corner than he was the year before; he may occasionally dress up in women's clothes or agree to be Daddy, but the superhero clique has formed and the doll corner is becoming a women's room. For their part, four-year-old girls may intermittently exchange domestic roles for Wonderwoman and Supergirl, but Mother and Baby reign supreme and will continue to do so throughout the kindergarten year.

The atmosphere in the doll corner changes dramatically among five- and six-year-olds. "They are bored," say some adults. "They've had enough doll-corner play." The doll corner, in fact, is entering its final phase, in which girls and boys try to end lingering confusion about the roles they play, roles they will now examine in a predominantly social context.

Though the girls officiate in the doll corner, the presence or absence of boys determines the character of the play. The more cohesive the boys' group, the more disruptive is its doll-corner play; paradoxically, "good" behavior is most often found among the least mature boys. As the superhero dominates boys' fantasy play, the girls turn to dramatic plots that eliminate boys and bring in more sisters and princesses.

Boys set the tone and girls follow on parallel paths. Both seek a new *social* definition for "boy" and "girl." They search everywhere for clues, hoping to create separate and final images. Society supplies Barbie dolls and Star Wars, but the children invent equally interesting symbols by themselves.

In the class described in this book, for example, you hop to get your milk if you are a boy and skip to the paper shelf if you are a girl. Boys clap out the rhythm of certain songs; girls sing louder. Boys draw furniture inside four-story haunted houses; girls put flowers in the doorways of cottages. Boys get tired of drawing pictures and begin to poke and shove; girls continue to draw.

The observer can report what it looks like, but the mystery remains intact. Adults may approve or disapprove of certain behaviors and gather explanations from psychologists, but the children watch one another and synchronize their movements. It is the most exciting game in town, though not everyone knows what game is being played. The instruction starts on the first day of school, and the lessons are recorded in *Boys and Girls*.

The lessons are of another sort for me. This year I have tried to examine boys' play with more objectivity than in the past. The tape recorder is my disciplinarian, bidding me to reconsider each evening the talk of the day. While transcribing from the tape, I have time to hear between the quickly spoken lines. The margins of my journal fill with speculations and questions, and, the next day, curiosity makes me a more patient observer.

If I have not yet learned to love Darth Vader, I have at least made some useful discoveries while watching him at play. As I interrupt less, it becomes clear that boys' play is serious drama, not morbid mischief. Its rhythms and images are often discordant to me, but I must try to make sense of a style that, after all, belongs to half the population of the classroom.

It is easier said than done. The further away a boy moves from fantasy play, the more I appreciate him. Thus, while appearing to value play, I seem to admire boys most when they are not playing as young boys play. It is a conflict I must face, because superhero play has increased in the past decade, and begins at an earlier age.

The children are more comfortable with the arrangement than I am. That which they accept at face value, I must analyze and justify. Perhaps if I study what they teach one another, I can learn to celebrate with them the images they value most. The image they are quickest to promote and defend is separation by fantasy.

1 Social action in kindergarten is contained in dramatic plots. Since the characters create the plot, actors must identify themselves. In the doll corner, if a plumber arrives, then a pipe has just broken; the appearance of a schoolteacher signals that the children are about to receive a lesson.

The four girls in the doll corner have announced who they are: Mother, Sister, Baby, Maid. To begin with, then, there will be cooking and eating, crying and cleaning. Charlotte is the mother because, she tells the others, she is wearing the silver shoes. Leadership often goes to the child who is most confident about the meaning of symbols.

> Karen: I'm hungry. Wa-a-ah!
> Charlotte: Lie down, baby.
> Karen: I'm a baby that sits up.
> Charlotte: First you lie down and sister covers you
> and then I make your cereal and *then* you sit up.
> Karen: Okay.

Teddy watches the scene as he fills up the number board for the second time. Charlotte returns his stare and says, "You can be the father." He inserts the last two tiles and enters the doll corner.

"Are you the father?" Charlotte asks.

"Yes."

"Put on the red tie." She doesn't know Teddy's name yet, but she can tell him what to wear because she is mother.

The girls look pleased. "I'll get it for you, honey," Janie says in a falsetto voice. She is the maid. "Now, don't that baby look pretty? This is your daddy, baby." Teddy begins to set the table, matching cups and saucers as deliberately as he did the tiles on the number board.

Abruptly the mood changes. Andrew, Jonathan, Jeremy, and Paul rush in, fingers shooting. "We're robbers. Do you got any gold?"

"No," Charlotte says, stirring an empty pot.

Jeremy climbs on the refrigerator and knocks over several

cartons of plastic food. "Put up your hands. You're going to jail!"

"We're telling!" The girls stomp out in search of me or my assistant, Mrs. Brandt.

Cops and robbers is off to an early start. The first week of kindergarten is usually uneventful as children cautiously decide what they can expect from one another and from the teacher. They want to know with whom they will play and how free is free play. The four robbers in the doll corner are already a team, having practiced being bad guys in nursery school. They are impatient to test classroom limits; but, mindful of my resolve to study their behavior, I sidestep the issue.

"You can't keep spoiling the play in the doll corner, Andrew," I say with affected calmness.

"It's not spoiled. It's gooder this way."

"Only if the girls agree that it's better. Tell me what you were playing and let's see if it makes a good story for me to write down."

"Cops and robbers?"

"Sure. If you tell me what the cops and robbers do, I'll write down your words and that will be a story. Then we'll act it out at piano time just the way we did 'The Three Billy Goats Gruff' yesterday."

Storytelling is easy to promote when there is a tangible connection to play. Andrew's story completes the interrupted scene in the doll corner:

> The four robbers are shooting people in the middle of the night. Then they had enough shooting, so they snuck up on the house and said, "Put up your hands!" Then the robbers brought the good people to jail. Then they went back to steal the money. Then they went to their hiding places.

Later, with the class seated around the sixteen-foot circle we use as a stage, I read Andrew's story and ask for actors.

"I have to be the boss of the robbers," Andrew says, "because it's my story."

Jeremy waves his arms wildly. "I'm a robber!" The boys who volunteer for Andrew's play all want to be robbers.

"Who will be the good people?" I ask.

Several girls' hands tentatively go up. Out of the doll corner, a girl can afford to be less rigid.

The next day, Paul and Jonathan follow Andrew's lead in storytelling as they do in play, but he is not chosen to be the "boss." This, the children begin to realize, is one of the many advantages of authorship.

> We sneaked up in the house. Then we put the good guys in jail. Then we killed some of the good guys. Then the four bad guys got some money and some jewels. (Paul)

> When the robbers were looking for gold they went to every house and they said, "Do you have any gold?" If the people said yes, then they took it, and if they said no, then they said, "You better get some or we'll put you in jail." So they had to put some in jail, but not all. (Jonathan)

Charlotte is no more influenced by the boys' stories than by their play. Her story is a doll-corner idyll, and she is, of course, the "pretty bunny."

> Once there was four kittens and they found a pretty bunny. Then they went to buy the bunny some food and they fed the baby bunny and then they went on a picnic.

Every year, the girls begin with stories of good little families, while the boys bring us a litany of superheroes and bad guys. This kind of storytelling is an adjunct of play; it follows existing play and introduces new ideas for the future. Language development and creative dramatics may be on *my* mind, but the children take over the story-plays for a more urgent matter; to inform one another of the preferred images for boys and girls.

Teddy tells his first story at the end of the week. The boys'
response is immediate and strong.

> Once upon a time there was this little boy and his
> name was Pretty. They called him Pretty because he
> was so pretty. His name was really Hansel. There
> was this sister. He didn't know he had a sister. The
> mother and father told him and then they had candy
> and then they went for a walk.

Andrew, Jonathan, and Paul explode with laughter. "He
calls him Pretty!" "Ugh!" "Pre-e-tty!"

"He can call him that if he wants," Charlotte says.

"No he can't!" shouts Andrew. "Not if he's a boy he can't."

"It's Teddy's story," I add. "He didn't tell you what to say."

Teddy is not insulted, only curious. He smiles at the boys,
who continue to make faces. Teddy's use of "pretty" crosses
over into female territory, a subject he will learn about from
boys, who care more about boundary lines than do the girls.

"Anyway, his name is Hansel. Just call him that." Teddy
looks at the boys as he speaks.

"Are you sure, Teddy?" I ask.

"Yeah. I'm sure."

2 Franklin is one of Teddy's two friends. He
lives a distance from this university community and Teddy sees him only in school. He is
as dark as Teddy is fair, exuberant as Teddy is solemn. "Ah
needs tha' hammer, boy," he tells Teddy at the wood-bench.
They make boats nearly every day. When their hammers clang
in unison, Franklin says, "Me and you workin' men, huh!"

Besides making boats and painting them, Franklin draws
pictures of houses and cars. He acknowledges that he is the
only boy in this class whose first choice during free play is

painting and drawing. "The girls mostly likes to color, 'cept for me," he says.

The girls do, in fact, like to color. Throughout the scheduled playtimes—forty five minutes in the morning and thirty minutes in the afternoon—plus all the incidental times between activities, the art tables are filled with girls and deftly avoided by boys. If I insist that the boys sit down and draw, they animate their volcanoes and space wars with exploding noises, as if they have jumped inside the pictures. Teddy comes more often to the tables now because he wants to be with Franklin.

Robert is Teddy's other friend and game partner. They play checkers, tic-tac-toe, dominoes, Curious George, and Cat and Mouse. Once in a while they build something in the block area, but then Robert suggests they attach what they have built to Andrew's spaceship, and Teddy leaves. Superhero play makes him timid—a small inconvenience indoors, where there is so much to do, but a major problem on the playground.

"I don't have any friends," he says when we go outside.

"Sure you do, Teddy. What do you feel like playing?"

"I want to go inside."

"What's Franklin doing?"

"They're playing Jaws."

"Let's go see who's in the sandbox."

"Never mind."

Teddy likes the sandbox and the maze of poles, chutes, and ladders that cover the playground. When he and the others dig holes and climb heights, there are no differences between the sexes. But then Mother and Sister stop to gather leaves and seeds, and the boys unleash *their* powerful creatures, who run into one another at such exhilarating speeds that the girls move away. Girls like to be chased, but the boys' impulsive movements worry them.

Teddy cannot ignore these dramatic contrasts. A compelling herdlike instinct propels the boys into large-scale maneuvers unknown among the girls, who go off in twos and threes. Super friends and enemies blend into a collage of shooting, chasing, and complaining, but the message is "We are boys" to some and "I am an outsider" to others.

Teddy is reluctant to join, yet not content to remain apart. My sympathy and suggestions serve only to focus on his loneliness. At five, the feeling of being an outsider strikes with new impetus. Outsideness is now seen in terms of membership in a boys' or a girls' group.

It is drawing time. Mrs. Brandt has sent Andrew, Jeremy, and Paul to a table to draw because of an overlong noisy argument in the block area. They see the act as a punishment and recover status by scribbling on both sides of their paper.

Franklin pays no attention to the newcomers to his table. He is making a Halloween picture. "This is a hunna house," he says.

"Honey house? Honey, honey, honey house!" The boys scream and laugh and pound the table. They keep repeating Franklin's words until he is laughing, too.

"Ah ain' tol' no joke! This is a real hunna house wit' a ghos'!"

Teddy, who is seated beside him, shouts, "It's a *haunted* house! *Haunted!*"

"Yeah. Haunet," Franklin agrees.

The boys look at Franklin as though seeing him for the first time. Teddy reddens and speaks again with uncharacteristic loudness. "Franklin sure does make a nice house. See, it has furniture inside. He makin' a real house!"

In Teddy's passionate appeal, he directs the boys to consider not only Franklin's house but also Franklin's manner of speaking. He uses Franklin's rhythm, his inflection, and even a piece of his grammar. Teddy has found a hero.

3 Suddenly the boys are drawing haunted houses. Cars, volcanoes, and space wars are temporarily set aside; unpredictably, Franklin's house has become a rallying banner. Jaws served a similar purpose on the playground, but Franklin's house is more of a private ceremony. Symbols imposed by society sometimes cause dissension, as if the children are stimulated in ways they cannot fathom. Their own creations, simple and direct, bring unity and contentment.

Franklin's houses, which he has been drawing for several days, have four floors, including an attic and a basement. There is usually a train set and a tent in the basement, a kitchen and a dining room on the first floor, beds on the second, and chairs in the attic. Starting in the basement, he draws upward, furnishing each floor as he goes.

A house seems an unlikely selection as a male ritual. Houses are usually drawn by girls. However, Franklin calls his a "haunted house" and uses a ruler. Rulers are "working men's" tools, and weapons in the arsenal of sticks boys wave, poke, and shoot at one another. The ruler is very masculine.

The girls notice that something is going on and leave the doll corner and art tables to watch the unusual specter of eight boys sprawled on the floor drawing fully equipped houses. After a close examination, Charlotte returns to her painting of a girl with yellow hair and paints a house next to the girl. Unlike Franklin's cutaway view, her house reveals two faces looking out of an upstairs window and has a flower on each side of the door. Several girls at the art table copy Charlotte's house, varying only the number of flowers at the doorway.

The room is quiet. Noise comes in hills and valleys in the kindergarten. Even a Star Wars drama will eventually wind down, the players scattering into gentler pursuits. Calmness follows excitement in natural rhythms, the mood shifting back into restless gear as increased physical tensions generate new fantasies. My own measure of contentment and anxiety follows close upon the mood of the boys.

Andrew runs into the empty doll corner and begins dumping clothes from shelves and hangers onto the floor while Franklin watches.

"Y'all playin' house?" Franklin asks.

Andrew looks around quickly, self-consciously borrowing Franklin's patois. "This gonna be a spaceship. Y'wanna play?"

There are six boys in the doll corner. It is the first time they have been there without girls. Gregory and Ned totter and clump about in high heels, their arms stuck awkwardly into unfastened dresses. They giggle and screech and stumble into the other boys, who laugh and pull them down.

Andrew darts questioning glances my way as he surveys the mess: naked dolls face down under the crib, chairs overturned, hats and shoes heaped on piles of dresses and dishes. There is a moment of stillness and then Jeremy drags the oven to the middle of the floor.

"This is the computer terminal," he declares.

"Put it over here," says Paul. He picks up the fallen chairs and sets them in two straight rows. The oven is now covered by the shoe rack. Andrew turns two shoes back and forth and speaks into a silver slipper:

"Pilot to crew, pilot to crew, ready for landing. Snow Planet down below."

"Watch out! It exploded!"

"Darth Vader is coming!"

"*Millennium Falcon*, where are you?"

"E-e-k! B-e-e-p! Erk! Erk!"

"Get the light sabers!"

Andrew runs to the wood-bench. He grabs two long sticks and slams them on the painting table. "Quick! Emergency! Where's the red paint?"

Mary Ann looks doubtful but hands him her paintbrush.

"Thanks, miss, I won't forget this." He paints a red tip on each stick and rushes back to the doll corner. "Am I too late?"

"Just in time. Darth Vader found us, but we got away. Wait, he might be invisible." Paul kicks a pile of clothes.

All the while, Franklin has been turning an unseen steering wheel, making a siren sound and staring through squinty eyes. "M-m-m . . . M-m-m . . . Darth Vader, he escapin'! Follow me, men. Ah knows his plan. M-m-m . . . K-k-k . . . P-p-ah-ah! Ah blowed his ship to pieces. He back on the Death Star."

The boys gaze at Franklin in admiration. Ned repeats Franklin's words softly, to himself: "He back on the Death Star."

The girls don't care what goes on in the doll corner when they are not there. It is not a place so much as an idea ready to be adapted. Right now the girls are in the block area building a zoo. They have named the four rubber lions Mother, Father, Sister, and Baby and put them in a two-story house. Girls tame lions by putting them into houses. Boys conquer houses by sending them into space.

4   Once upon a time there was a girl named Snow White and there was a prince and he loved that girl. And he always loved her like a rose. He loved her so so so much better than the time before. And one day they met each other at the pond and they saw seven dwarfs.

The boys react on cue to Charlotte's prince who loved Snow White like a rose. "I won't be a prince. No way!" Andrew sticks out his tongue. "It's disgusting!"

"It certainly is not disgusting, Andrew," I say.

"*He's* disgusting if he says that," counters Charlotte.

"I'll be the prince," Teddy says. The boys, having made their point, say nothing further and the story is performed without incident.

Later, at the painting table:

"I wonder, why do you suppose boys never tell stories about princes and princesses?" I ask.

"They like rougher games than girls," Janie says.

"Couldn't it be a rough prince?"

The girls look at me in surprise. "Princes are never rough," they answer in unison.

Mary Ann is painting a row of red tulips. "Boys don't like to be fancy. Not kings or queens."

Charlotte nods. "Princes are good guys. The boys like bad guys."

"I like to be a prince," says Teddy from the easel.

"Sure. Some boys do," I say quickly.

He looks around doubtfully. "But not all the time I don't."

"Teddy, just because Andrew made such a fuss, you don't need to change your mind," I tell him in a whisper.

He avoids my gaze and continues to make random swirls with the paintbrush, the colors mixing into a grayish brown. He doesn't want to hear the adult feminine point of view, but when Charlotte speaks again, he looks up with interest.

"Here's what I think," Charlotte states definitively. "They don't want to be fancy because girls *do*. They just like to be not the same as us."

5   This morning the girls are painting their nails silver. Clarice bought a bottle of silver disco nail polish at the fourth-grade flea market and the girls perform their solemn rites, two at a time, under the doll-corner table. Teddy approaches, then hesitates, uncertain about the scene he is watching.

"Don't come in, Teddy," Charlotte says. "Only girls are allowed."

This is the first time Teddy has been rejected by the girls. All the boys stay out, and so do I. I would like to confiscate the nail polish but cannot think of a sensible reason for doing so. There seems to be no difference between putting on nail polish and putting on high heels; yet I am vaguely disturbed by the hushed excitement, the air of secrecy in the doll corner.

I tell myself young girls need to identify collectively as females; opposition to these ceremonies only makes them more desirable. Even so, I keep hoping we have no visitors while the nail polishing proceeds. As in all areas of uncertainty, I vacillate between the evidence continually provided by the children's behavior, and my need to conform to conventional standards and opinions.

Barbie dolls affect me in a similar way, and Charlotte thinks she knows why. When Karen, still wearing the silver polish, brings her Barbie doll the next day, every girl is magnetized around the doll, causing the suspension of all other activities. On each face is the same happy, glazed look that pervaded the nail-polishing fete.

"Are we allowed to bring Barbie dolls?" Karen asks, handing me a note that reads: "I couldn't talk Karen out of bringing the Barbie doll. Do you mind?"

"Why does Mother think I'll mind?"

"She says you won't like it."

"I know why," Charlotte says. "Because it has breasts."

Mildly shocked, I am immediately certain that Charlotte is right. "No, I don't mind. You can play with it."

A full-figured female doll excites every girl in the class, and I am as little pleased as when Andrew runs about waving his light saber.

The girls depart for the doll corner and concentrate on dressing and undressing Barbie. They stare at her the way boys stare at their superhero figures, standing her on the table, moving her arms and legs in slow motion. Their customary dramatic outpouring is replaced by scant utterances and private smiles.

"Can we bring Barbie to the playground?" Karen asks.

"I'd rather you didn't," I reply. "She'll cause a fuss out there."

"Oh, please!"

"No, Karen. Everyone will be just sitting around watching you dress the doll."

"Then can we stay in?" Mary Ann pleads.

"I'm afraid not. Mrs. Brandt and I are both going out."

I hear my ungenerous tones. I am annoyed when the girls

expose my ambivalence about certain matters of female sexuality in the classroom.

Teddy observes the Barbie-doll tableau but does not enter the doll corner. He can see that this is not ordinary doll-corner play where femaleness comes in comfortable doses. "Pretend we're sisters and a prince wants to marry us" is reasonably safe coming from little girls wrapped in curtains. All Teddy needs to do in that scenario is put on the beaded black vest and take the baby for a walk.

With the Barbie doll, there is no role for Teddy. The message is clear: Find something to do that boys do. He marches into the block area and begins to build a tower.

"What do you want to make?" asks Robert.

"This is a space shuttle," answers Teddy in a gruff voice. "I'm Luke."

This is the first time I have heard Teddy identify himself as a superhero.

6 On Halloween morning Teddy stuffs his new Superman costume into his cubby and waits at the door for Franklin. A moment later his friend walks in wearing a sheet.

"Where your costume at?" His eyes explore every part of Teddy. "You ain' got nothin' to wear?"

"Are you a ghost?" Teddy asks.

"Boo! Ah scarin' the girls. Boo!" Waving his arms through the holes in the sheet, Franklin runs through the room and then he returns to Teddy. "Hey, you wanna be a ghos'? My mama, she say if the sheet too long, rip it in two. Okay?"

Teddy nods and Franklin brings Mrs. Brandt the sheet, giving detailed directions for making two ghosts out of one. Teddy blushes with excitement and, once the sheet is on, he follows behind Franklin silently, letting his friend make the appropriate noises.

However, after lunch, Teddy tells a ghost story. It is his first story since "a boy named Pretty."

> Once upon a time there was a ghost trying to find someone to scare. The people came to scare the ghost, but they didn't see him. He was invisible. Suddenly a great storm came, but it didn't happen to anyone. Then a phantom came. He came and blew a great storm. It blew the people away. Suddenly a ghost sound came. It scared the phantom away. The men came to try to shoot the phantom, but they couldn't find him.

Before going home, Teddy puts on the sheet again and runs into the doll corner. "Boo!"

"No ghosts in here, Teddy," Charlotte says. "Do you want to be a prince? We're playing Cinderella."

"Okay." He removes the sheet and begins to arrange the shoes on the rack while Cinderella, Snow White, and a ballet dancer adjust their costumes in front of the mirror.

Charlotte, in her tutu, is Mother. "Sisters, go out and get macaroni and chocolate cake because the prince is coming. And don't forget to wear your silver slippers to the ball."

Halloween is easy for a girl. No matter what costume she wears, she can still be the mother, sister, or baby. Boys are far less adaptable in fantasy play. A boy in a Superman costume is Superman until he removes his costume. "I'm Superman" in ordinary play is a fleeting commitment, but a Halloween superhero costume is a lengthy call to action.

The day after Halloween, Charlotte tells a Cinderella story and Teddy receives another lesson from the boys:

> Once upon a time there lived a princess called Cinderella who was beautiful as ever, and another sister who was ugly in rags. One day the beautiful princess went to a ball. The ball was filled with golden flowers. Some of them fell in her hands. She saw a prince there. She wanted to marry him. So

they got married. The prince gave her a bunny. And they lived happily ever after.

Teddy takes the role of the prince, as he did in the doll corner, but when I read the part about getting married, the boys are more disruptive than ever.

"Really now, boys, why the silly business? What's wrong with getting married?"

"He'll have to *kiss* her!" yells Andrew.

In the boys' dual school language, marriage and kissing are on the girls' list. Initially the boys act as if these words embarrass them, but the response, once established, becomes a ritualized part of their behavior.

Six months earlier, in nursery school, references to marriage and kissing could be made without a stir. Suddenly the boys have polarized the language of play and storytelling. Andrew will hold Mary Ann's hand on a class walk and may even say he intends to marry her, but he wants a different image for fantasy play.

"Pretend we're boys and we're storm troopers," he says to Paul on the playground.

"Why do you say 'Pretend we're boys'?" I ask him. "You really *are* boys."

"I know. It means pretend we're *this* kind of boys. Tough boys."

7   "Andrew is the strongest boy in the class," Robert tells me one day.

        "How do you know that?" I ask.

"Well, I just know. I don't know how except that he's strong. Even though I'm the tallest." Robert ponders this possible contradiction. "But I know he's stronger than Paul, and Paul is stronger than me."

"How can you be so sure who is stronger?"

"Andrew can beat everyone," Robert continues. "He can wrestle everyone—every boy."

"But we don't allow wrestling. Where did you see all this wrestling? At Andrew's house?"

"No, I didn't see them wrestle. But Andrew told me. I mean, he didn't tell me, but someone told me."

Robert cannot explain why he thinks Andrew is the strongest boy. Actually, Andrew is a small boy, almost the smallest boy in the class. He is a runner, not a wrestler. He is also the number-one spinner of superhero fantasies and organizes most of the superhero play.

Robert wishes he could be like Andrew and create strong and powerful images. This desire is expressed more in Robert's stories than in his play. Though he runs with the boys in the playground and builds with them in the blocks, he still likes to play in the doll corner. For the time being, Robert solves this dilemma by casting himself in the role of a naughty puppy in the doll corner and Superdog in his stories.

> Once upon a time Superman and Wonderwoman
> and Superdog went on a walk. When they went on a
> walk they saw a monster. Wonderwoman and
> Superman shot the monster with Superman's gun.
> Superdog brought him to jail.

Initially, Robert's stories were gentle tales about "a little boy named Jack" who performs no heroic deeds:

> Once upon a time there was a little boy named
> Jack. One time he went to the giant's house. When
> he got there he went inside. The giant was sleeping.

As Robert listens to other boys' stories, he learns how to give himself a grander image:

> Once there was Wolfman. And then the real
> Frankenstein came. And then he called Dracula.
> Dracula told him to bring Luke Skywalker to suck
> his blood. So he did and he died. Then Superdog

made him come alive. Then Superdog made all the
people come alive that Dracula killed.

Expertly Robert repeats the "party line," though he has no
television set at home. All his information comes from other
boys.

Thirty years ago, no child in my kindergarten had a television set. Younger boys watched older boys on the playground
and brought army games into the kindergarten. In pre-super-
hero days, battle stations were fortified by "army men" and
"enemies." Davy Crockett and Jesse James crossed fire while
Tonto and the Lone Ranger lassoed nameless outlaws and
took them to jail. All the good guys and bad guys got killed
until the recess bell rang. The raucous display of power carried little boys away from female influence into a separate
world of male heroes.

Every year, the boys search and find their means to the
same end. The names of the heroes change, but the action is
the same. The result is a widening gap between boys and girls.

8   At piano time we sometimes talk instead of
    sing. One such discussion begins with the
    mention of separate lines for boys and girls
and ends with their sitting on opposite sides of the circle.

The discussion itself concerns the best way to choose a daily
leader, but even the brief reference to single sex lines creates a
spontaneous mass response.

> Jonathan: Why can't we have a boys' line and a girls'
> line like that other class?
> Teacher: They were going to the bathroom—and
> older boys and girls go to separate bathrooms. We
> have our own toilets.
> Jonathan: Can't we go to theirs?
> Teacher: No, but you will in first grade.
> Charlotte: That reminds me. I want leaders to be

from cubbies and not from the list on the wall,
because then it'll be quicker to be your turn again.

Teacher: Why is it quicker to go cubby by cubby
instead of name by name from the list?

Charlotte: Because when you go down the list and
the last person they would have to wait a little
longer than the cubby way.

Paul: She's right. Because there are not so many
cubbies. There are more names.

Teacher: Doesn't each name have a cubby?

Clarice: He means the names are littler than the
cubbies.

Charlotte: So you could look better at the cubbies.

Andrew: No, it's the same thing. Everyone has a
cubby.

Charlotte: Yeah, but the list is longer.

Teacher: Let's do this. I'll call every name on the list.
When I call your name, stand in front of your
cubby. (There is an attitude of suspense as the
children fill up the spaces in front of each cubby.)
Now, let's count the list names. (We count to
twenty four.) Okay, count cubbies. (We count
again to twenty four.)

Paul: It takes longer to call the names.

Teacher: Charlotte, we counted twenty four names
and twenty four cubbies. Do you still think you'll
get your turn faster if we go by cubbies?

Charlotte: I do a little bit.

Mary Ann: No it won't, Charlotte. It'll be the same.

Jeremy: It *will* be shorter.

Andrew: It has to be the same.

Jeremy: It can't be, because they're both different.
You can even see the cubbies faster.

Mary Ann: No. See, it's really like the same thing
except for being in a different place.

Charlotte: It really is shorter by cubbies. Just *look*.
Can't you see your cubby quicker?

Teacher: How many agree with Charlotte, that you'll
have your turn to be leader sooner if we go cubby
by cubby? (Every hand but two goes up.) How

many want to make the change? (Every hand goes up.)

As the discussion ends, Teddy and I become aware, at the same time, that the circle is now divided into a boys' side and a girls' side, with Teddy in the girls' section. This took place when the children reassembled after going to their cubbies. Teddy looks around the circle, puzzled, hesitating between kneeling and standing. Then he gets up and moves to the boys' side. Nothing is said by either group, but whenever they come to the circle from this time on, the children separate according to sex.

I mention the matter one day as we begin a game:

> Teacher: When we come to the circle now, the boys sit on one side and the girls on the other. Then when we play circle games it's always a whole bunch of boys who get turns and then a whole bunch of girls.
>
> Mary Ann: You could pick the whole bunch of girls first.
>
> Teacher: I think it would be better if we were all mixed together as we used to be.
>
> Charlotte: This is better, because what if a girl's hair is too short and someone thinks she's a boy but then they can see she's sitting with the girls?
>
> Jeremy: Or if someone's in disguise but then you know by where they're sitting.
>
> Mary Ann: If they're in disguise they could try to fool you.
>
> Jeremy: Then you'll know it's the other side from where they're sitting.

The children are swift to rationalize any separate-sex arrangement. All opportunities to make oneself distinctly feminine or masculine are seized upon: *If I am doing something only boys do, then I must be a boy.*

9 It is possible to segregate almost any activity by sex. We are at the piano singing "The Crawdad Hole" when Franklin gets up on one knee and claps out the rhythm of the song. His pose is country-western singer, eyes narrowed, imaginary cowboy hat dipping over one eyebrow. After watching for a moment, Andrew rises and assumes the same posture. He is quickly followed by Robert, Paul, and Jeremy. By the third verse, most of the boys are balancing on one knee. The girls do not join them but begin singing louder until they are almost shouting.

A day later Charlotte and Mary Ann, side by side on the circle, turn to face each other during "Jenny Jenkins" and begin a complex cross-clapping routine. Soon several pairs of girls are clapping each other's hands and thighs in alternating rhythms. It is an intricate style of clapping and few boys can do it. Andrew calls it "girl's clapping," which implies that only girls are supposed to clap this way.

Andrew and his friends mimic the cross-clapping and instantly succumb to pushing and pounding one another. They seldom remain calm in contact activities; push leads to shove, and the focus of the activity changes. Besides being enjoyable, the pummeling serves as a camouflaging ploy. Boys often cover up real or imagined deficiencies by substituting other behaviors.

Many five-year-old boys, for example, are awkward when it comes to skipping, whereas girls have begun to skip as naturally as they walk. During "Skip to My Lou" Jonathan trips twice as he starts to skip, so he switches to a hop. Adding a touch of bravado, he falls down on every fourth hop. The boys' faces light up; they see the logic in hopping to avoid skipping. (Later, as if to justify the act, Jonathan hops to get his milk. His method is immediately taken up by the other boys until several dropped cartons bring an official halt.)

Ned shares the concern most boys have about their public image. He is good at skipping and enjoys it, but he now wonders if hopping is more masculine. He skips around the circle at double speed, masking his desire to skip by adding a competitive factor. Franklin joins the hoppers though he is a competent skipper. If skipping meant as much to him as drawing, he would not alter his performance to suit group norms.

It is Teddy's turn. Usually he blushes through a timid trot in lieu of a skip, but this time Teddy leaps into the circle just as Franklin starts his second hop around. He catches up to his friend in a few running hops and pulls him down, both boys shrieking with laughter.

Teddy is still laughing when he returns to the circle, and Jonathan, encouraged by Teddy's first public display of roughness, begins to wrestle with him. "Stop that, Jonathan!" says an offended Teddy, obviously not ready to allow someone else to initiate roughness. Jonathan's presumption is of the sort that keeps Teddy from joining the superhero games in the playground.

If Teddy's pose as a hopper aligns him with the boys, his attitude toward outdoor running puts him on the girls' side. They prefer short sprints and limited body contact during and after a chase. Should a monster (always a boy) chase them, he must follow girls' rules: no forceful capturing. The boys are willing to accommodate the eccentricities of girls but expect other boys to understand the need for rough play.

It is a matter of social image mixed with private fantasy. Boys and girls are equally capable as walkers and runners; yet the characters in a girl's drama are more likely to walk or skip, while the boys' characters receive additional practice in running and falling.

"Paul pushed me down," Jeremy complains. "He choked me."

"I told you not to play that way," I reply. "Someone could get hurt."

"We're storm troopers," Paul explains.

"Don't run into each other that way," I insist, but their faraway looks show they are back in action. There will be more tears and anger—it is unavoidable. They act out pictures in their minds in which characters are always in motion, coming to a stop only against another male body.

Boys are no more fond of getting hurt than girls. They cry as much if they are knocked down, but they return to the drama

20

before the tears dry. The need to be part of the chase is stronger than hurt feelings or scraped knees.

Which has come first, the fantasy or the physical inclination? It is as difficult to make distinctions between fantasy and physical release as between "good" and "bad," the names of the two teams who chase and shoot each other. For kindergarten boys, fantasy and flight are synonymous. Running and leaping are what they like best, and nothing else makes them feel more distinctly the opposite of the girls.

10
Once there was Luke Skywalker, and Darth Vader cut off his hand. Then IG88 froze Han Solo. Then Luke killed the storm troopers. Then Hammerhead shot Han Solo, but he was not dead, only bleeding a lot. (Jonathan)

Jonathan has not seen *Star Wars* and is always eager to increase his knowledge. "This is Boss's spaceship," he says, pointing to a drawing he has just made on his lunch place mat.

"Boss don't have no spaceship," Franklin tells him.

"Well, anyway, who's he the boss of?" Jonathan asks.

"Snaggletooth. And Snaggletooth, he not anybody's boss."

The brochure that accompanied Andrew's latest Star Wars doll shows "Boss" to be a bounty hunter named Bossk. Whether he is really Snaggletooth's boss is not important in these conversations. The appearance of knowing is as good as the truth itself. Certainty is valued over accuracy.

"The At-At is the boss of Boss, and Boss is the boss of Hammerhead."

"You mean At-At drivers."

Details of the Star Wars story are a major fact of classroom life this year. Half of the boys have seen *Star Wars* and *The Empire Strikes Back* and they teach what they know to the other boys. There is enough chapter and verse to add a new twist to the serialized version acted out daily.

The talk at lunch often examines the fine points of the story. This day the hierarchy of bosses is being analyzed.

"Storm troopers are the boss of Imperial storm troopers, and Imperial storm troopers are the boss of the At-At drivers," Jeremy reports. "And Boba Fett is the boss of the storm troopers."

"Darth Vader is the boss of Boba Fett."

"The Empire is the boss of Darth Vader!"

"But not Obi-Wan Kenobi."

The names roll out importantly, joining other incantations around the table: "Darth Vader . . . Chewbacca . . . Han Solo . . . Luke Skywalker . . . Death Star. . ." No story receives more attention from the boys or gives greater pleasure in the telling. Sometimes a girl is drawn in, though her facts may differ from the boys'.

"Princess Leia is Luke's sister," Charlotte notes.

Andrew rejects the idea. "Uh-uh. Princess Leia is the boss of the good guys. Then Luke."

Teddy takes a turn. "Luke is the boss of Han, and Han is the boss of Chewbacca, and Chewbacca is the boss of the other men." Teddy is one of those who has not seen the movie, but today he brought a tiny replica of Darth Vader to school.

"Who is Chewbacca the boss of?" asks Charlotte.

"C3PO. And C3PO is the boss of R2D2." Franklin's rapid delivery of these magical symbols is in sharp contrast to his hesitancy in number games. Another change I am suddenly aware of in this conversation is his increasing adaptation to the standard speech of the classroom. "And R2D2 is the boss of R5D4, and R5D4 is the boss of R8D12."

"I can't remember about Power Droid," Mary Ann says to Andrew.

"He's a bad guy. He's 5X7."

"He ain't nobody's boss," Franklin adds.

"He's just 2-1," says Jonathan.

"You mean 2-1B," corrects Franklin. "He's the boss of FX7."

"Who are all these numbered people?" I ask. There is a chorus of excited voices, as if the mere mention of names endows the speaker with power.

"Rebel soldiers."

"Some are X-wing pilots."

"And rebel soldiers."

"And Y-wing."

"Z-wing."

"Ain't no Z-wing!"

"Jawas."

"They're good guys."

Now Franklin ties up the loose ends, giving Power Droid greater authority and placing him on the good side. "Sandman is the boss of the Jawas. Power Droid is the boss of the Sand People. Obi-Wan Kenobi is the boss of Power Droid. And Obi-Wan Kenobi don't have a boss."

The children think a great deal about leaders and followers. They are increasingly aware of the social order that exists beyond their control. This is particularly true of the boys, whose tendency to play in large groups makes the establishment of leaders essential. The huge Star Wars cast enables everyone to be someone's boss. In the playground after lunch, Jonathan announces that he is Sandman. "I'm the boss of the Jawas!" he says, although no one present is identified as the Jawas.

Besides a loosely defined leadership roster, Star Wars offers an easy transition between "good" and "bad." Characters move back and forth, in the children's version, without restrictions. Virtue and power are equally distributed, and opposing forces often end up in the same camp.

"Who is the strongest?" Charlotte asks. She has seen the movie but may distrust her memory, as Princess Leia was recently Cinderella's sister in the doll corner.

"Chewbacca is the strongest and nobody can't hurt him," Robert tells her.

"Uh-uh," Franklin disagrees. "Darth Vader. He's got the Force."

"They both are!"

"How 'bout Yoda?"

"Who's the boss of Yoda?"

"No one!"

The talk ends with the scales of power balanced. Chewbacca and Luke are equal to Darth Vader and the Empire. For all their daring, the boys arrange matters so no one loses. Star Wars, despite its commercial hokum, comes close to being a perfect vehicle for small boys' play. "Bad" is only a costume, running is the means to any end, and both sides win.

This year's class is particularly aware of the subtle difference between Star Wars and other superhero stories. They tag on "The good guys won" or "The bad guys won" to every Star Wars episode, though the conclusion may be unrelated to the plot. Jeremy, for example, announced a victory for the good guys after arranging it so they are incapacitated:

> Once upon a time Boba Fett was in his ship. Then
> Luke got his ship. Then Boba Fett took Luke to
> Darth Vader. He threw Luke in the Trash
> Compactor. He threw Han Solo in, too. They got
> frozen. The good guys won.

The boys have invented an ending that achieves the same effect as "They lived happily ever after." If it appears different—girls never let bad people win—it is because the boys are using camouflage again, disguising bad and good characters to make their differences unrecognizable. The boys won't take chances: What if a *real* bad guy happens to appear?

Charlotte asks Andrew, "What if the real Darth Vader came here?"

"He doesn't. He's only in space."

"But what if?"

"I'd get the real Luke. He'd cut his head off. He can do that."

Teddy interrupts, speaking quietly: "I might be Luke when I grow up."

Andrew examines Teddy's face. "You can't be the real Luke."

"I know. I mean a different Luke Skywalker but he looks the same."

"Oh," Andrew says.

Teddy grins in amazement. He has revealed his dream and been taken seriously by Andrew.

11   Luke Skywalker is much admired, but Darth Vader's name is uttered with awe. The bad guy always promises more power—or more freedom—than the good guy.

At three, Andrew discovered the "monster" on the nursery school playground. "Star Wars" was not yet in his vocabulary, and the Superman T-shirt he unfailingly wore was a pledge for the future.

His first stories told of a "great big big big monster purple and orange" that ate people and houses. Acted out, it was a nameless creature roaring around in hopes of scaring someone. The "someone," he found out, were girls. Even a four-year-old girl would act frightened or at least annoyed and run to the teacher with complaints.

Another thing he learned was that girls are never monsters. To be a monster, therefore, is to be instantly identifiable as a boy—a reassuring feeling even at three. Andrew's habit of bumping into other boys already made him seem different from girls, but "monster" was an official title. Superman, Batman, and Mighty Mouse soon joined the monster, but there were no visible differences. All heroes go "Bang! Bang!" Toy guns may not be allowed, but fingers and sticks are always available.

At some point before kindergarten the monsters acquire names—Dracula, Frankenstein, Wolfman—and it becomes even more difficult to tell them apart from the superheroes, a genre that is full of contradictions but makes perfect sense to the boys. Labeled "good," superheroes are nonetheless destructive. They save people while knocking down buildings; they jail bad and good people indiscriminately and set off explosives everywhere. Like monsters, they are uncompromisingly aggressive.

Both boys and girls avoid fantasy play that makes the distinction between heroes and villains irreversible, but in the boys' case, all characters behave as villains. "Cops and robbers" is in reality "robbers." Punishment is meted out to good people more often than to bad.

"Jails are supposed to be for bad people, Andrew," I comment one day. "You put the good people in jail."

"We're not bad people. We're bad guys," he explains. "Good people have to go to jail or they can become bad guys."

"Do you mean if they become bad guys they won't have to go to jail?"

"Right. But if they want to be good guys, they could put someone in jail, too."

"Oh. Then bad guys and good guys both have jails?"

"It depends who's the boss."

Good guy or bad guy, the aggressive tumble-and-wrestle of little boys is criticized by teachers from the first day of school. How can ideas that seem so good be considered bad so often?

Perhaps "good" means "bad" when fantasies are involved. It is good to think about powerful creatures and exciting to rehearse their pursuits. However, most adaptations in the classroom are quickly curtailed. A teacher may not use the word "bad," but the message is clear: Girls' fantasies are more acceptable. When girls run and scream, the absence of ambush and crossfire soothes the teacher's ruffled senses. The children see girls as good and find it difficult to characterize boys.

> Karen: Girls are nicer than boys.
> Janie: Boys are bad. Some boys are.
> Paul: Not bad. Pretend bad, like bad guys.
> Karen: My brother is really bad.
> Teacher: Aren't girls ever bad?
> Paul: I don't think so. Not very much.
> Teacher: Why not?

Paul: Because they like to color so much. That's one thing I know. Boys have to practice running.
Karen: And they practice being silly.

Karen is correct. A certain kind of uninhibited play is identified by both sexes as boys' play. One evening, for example, the children see a slapstick television commercial for a movie called *Stir Crazy*. It has no effect on the girls, but the next day the boys are converted into head-bobbing, floppy-armed clones of two Hollywood actors, one white and one black. The commercial shows them escaping from prison, behaving outrageously, and continually repeating, "That's right, we're bad, uh-huh, uh-huh."

Jonathan is first to make the commercial into a story, filling in a number of details that extend the concept of senseless behavior:

> One time there were stir-crazy men. One color was black and one color was white. One time a policeman put them in jail. Then he let them out. And then they said, "That's right, we're bad, uh-huh, uh-huh." The black guy punched a window glass and it broke and then they ate some gunpowder. "Oh, whee! That was good." Then he went to the gas city and smelled the gas. They took an ax and chopped their skin off and all their bones stuck out. Then the police put them back in jail. They said, "We're bad, uh-huh, uh-huh. You're bad, uh-huh, uh-huh."

The subject is badness, and each succeeding story is a list of frantic, silly behaviors. Andrew has his black man "swallow the shots in the gun" and "mash all the food in his hair." Jeremy's white man "cut off his clothes with a scissors and his hair and his toes, too." In Greg's story, "they pulled down the clock and the telephone wires and painted the rug black and white and mashed gasoline into the piano." Everyone keeps saying, "We're bad, we're bad."

"I don't care for these Stir Crazy stories," I say on the second day.

"They're funny."

"*We* like them."

"It's good!"

"Well, I don't agree. In fact, I don't want to write them down anymore."

"No fair," says Andrew. "The girls like them, too. I see them laughing." He reaches for what he thinks will be a convincing argument, since he sees me as lined up with the girls. "Ask Charlotte."

Charlotte responds immediately: "They *are* kind of funny."

"I'm sorry, boys. Since I have to do the writing, I'll have to decide for myself. I don't like them."

"Do you like Star Wars?" Teddy asks.

"Well, in Star Wars, people do try to think of good stories. It seems more serious to me, Teddy."

The room is silent. My arbitrary definition of a good story is a sudden change in the rules. They cannot understand why I object to stories that bring them so much pleasure, and I am unable to explain that a grownup man can write silly television commercials that make people laugh, but a little boy's interpretation of the same material is not welcome in school.

Children, however, are accustomed to unilateral rulings imposed from above. They soon learn that not all topics are debatable. This is unfortunate, because our best thinking—mine and theirs—often emerges from our biggest disagreements.

Teddy does not tell a Stir Crazy story. However, the following week he repeats the theme in the doll corner: "I'm stir crazy, watch out, I'm stir crazy!" He throws the Raggedy Ann doll and it just misses Clarice.

"Stop it, Teddy! I'm telling." She puts the doll back in the cradle, but Teddy grabs it again and throws it out of the doll corner. Then he collects the three remaining dolls and drops them into the trash pail, chanting, "Stir crazy, stupid crazy, throw the dolls in the garbage."

Teddy's scene is largely unnoticed by the children, but his shrill laughter brings me to his side. "What are you doing, Teddy?" I ask.

He is embarrassed. "Just playing." Red-faced and faintly

smiling, he picks up the dolls and takes them back. He looks like a boy who might be saying to himself, "That's right, I'm bad, uh-huh, uh-huh."

12

"What does 'stir crazy' mean?" I ask.
"It means 'crazy.'"
"If you jump around like this."
"No. You have to stir something. And then you get crazy."
"Like Clarice. She paints her hands."
"It's just 'stir crazy.' That's the name of it."
None of the children connects "stir crazy" with jail, though all the commercials take place in a jailhouse. They assume it means disorder of some kind, and Clarice's habit of stirring the paint and applying it to her hands comes easily to mind. Only a few girls deliberately paint their hands, but the majority share a love of splatter painting, glue-and-paint mixtures, and finger painting that puts more paint on them in a day than on the boys in a week. The girls often look as though they could be characters in a Stir Crazy story.

"How come you always do that, Clarice?" asks Franklin, who is careful to avoid paint on his hands.

"I like to mess around," she says, examining her painted fingers.

"That ain't messin' around. That's just plain mess by yourself. Messin' around means you botherin' somebody."

We have space for both kinds of mess—social and artistic. Our room is a large rectangle with a sixteen-foot circle painted in the middle. To the right, as you enter, are the art tables, easels, and sinks. To the left are the block and doll corners, separated by storage cabinets. Everything else fills in the area around the circle. Except for the art tables, equipment is moved periodically to solve specific problems. The present grouping, for example, resulted from complaints that the boys were monopolizing the blocks. The girls decided to move the doll corner next to the blocks so they would not have so far to walk. They are convinced this is the reason they do not capture their fair share of the blocks.

Free play occurs in two distinct environments: active social play on one side, and sedentary play on the other. Though there is usually a small group of girls in the doll corner, the overall impression is girls to the right and boys to the left. As in an orthodox synagogue, where men and women are separated by partitions, an invisible curtain hangs between the art tables and the rest of the room.

The girls spend most of their free time with art materials, and the boys spend theirs in the block area. Sand and water, the only free-form materials used more by the boys, are used as an extension of block play—actively, competitively. The mixing and molding of gooey substances, the application of colorful paints to multitextured surfaces—these quiet, comfortable pastimes are predominantely female activities. Why should so many boys appear wary of "artistic" experiences?

Appearances are deceiving; the boys themselves may be fooled. Once involved, they enjoy artwork as much as do the girls. It is not a matter of aesthetics or skill. The obstacles are time and patience, theirs and mine.

The boys begin most play periods on the floor with things that go fast, make noise, or rise up high. Table activities are postponed for fear time will run out before they have played enough. If a free period lasts sufficiently long, the boys will drift over to the tables, ready to sit down and make something. The biggest problem may be that I seldom allow free play to extend to that point.

The customary notion that "real" school happens at a table is hard to dispel. The thoughtful management of materials, design, and people in the block area seldom receives the same respect as table "work."

> Mary Ann: The boys don't like to work.
> Teacher: They're making a huge train setup right now.
> Mary Ann: That's not work. It's just playing.
> Teacher: When do girls play?

Charlotte: In the doll corner.
Teacher: How about at the painting table?
Mary Ann: That's work. You could call it play
  sometimes, but it's really called schoolwork.
Teacher: When is it work and when is it play?
Clarice: If you paint a real picture, it's work, but if
  you splatter or pour into an egg carton, then it's
  play.
Charlotte: It's mostly work, because that's where the
  teacher tells you how to do stuff.

I put the question of work versus play to the boys, who echo
the same views.

Teacher: The girls think the block area is for play
  and not for work. Is that what you think?
Jonathan: It *is* for play. But you could be a work
  person.
Teacher: If you're a work person, then what do you
  do in the blocks?
Andrew: Build very neatly and don't knock it down
  and don't play.
Teacher: How can you tell if you're working or
  playing?
Andrew: No Star Wars or superheroes. None of that
  stuff.
Paul: No shooting. And no robbers.
Jonathan: And no running.
Teacher: What else is work in this room?
Andrew: If you color or put your name on a thing. On
  a paper.
Paul: It has to be work if *you* tell us to do something.
Teacher: How about stories? Your own stories. Is
  that work?
Andrew: No, because that could be Star Wars or
  Superman.

The children are in agreement. Whatever involves fantasy
or creates a mess is play. Work is achieved sitting at a table,
with a teacher nearby giving orders. Girls sit more and there-

fore work more, while boys, who run more, are seen as playing more. These boys seem to run more than those in previous classes, and running always creates problems in a classroom. This year, however, it is clearer to me that rules outlawing running discriminate far more against boys than against girls. I am always trying to find a way to allow running without actually permitting it, an impossible goal. We need some sort of controlled running during free play that lets off steam without too much "messing around."

One day, as we watch the high school students on the outdoor track, it occurs to me we might have such a track in our classroom. This would not be for running games but rather for just plain running. I envision it being used freely during playtime in order to cut down on the frequent outbursts of chasing that occur during indoor play.

I tell the children my plan to tape a large oval track around the existing circle. A series of arrows will provide the first of two rules: one-way running and no pushing.

"Now," I say, finishing a roll of duct tape, "when you feel like running, no one will say 'Don't run.' Run for a while on the track and then go back to your activity."

The children are pleased, and I am certain I have solved the eternal problem of indoor running. On the first day, track behavior is a model of decorum. Boys and girls run in equal numbers and without incident. By the second day two differences are apparent: There are fewer girls running, and the boys act as if they are being chased. It is time for a third rule.

"People on a track do not chase each other," I warn. "They just run. If you need to pass someone, do it carefully. Hands off."

There is a lot of agreeable nodding, and several voices blurt out, "I wasn't chasing. It was Andrew."

By the third day the four girls who still run on the track have made a game of counting laps. Charlotte tells us, "I did eight all-arounds." The others do less, but it is not a competition. As the girls grow more controlled, the boys are more excited. We add a fourth rule: no shooting fingers.

"What's going on, boys? You never see the big boys shooting or grabbing on the track."

"We won't do it."

I watch their faces. They want to run in a serious manner, but the track is taking on a life of its own. By the fifth day many of the boys are on the track even before they remove their coats. They become armed superheroes the moment they see the track. Even worse, the arrows are having a hypnotic effect. Certain boys have difficulty leaving the track because they keep following the arrows.

"What's wrong, Teddy? Why are you crying?"

"Jonathan is Dracula. He's chasing me."

"Just step off the track, Teddy."

"The arrows!" he sobs helplessly.

"Jonathan! Stop this minute! Let Teddy off the track. Wait. *Everyone* leave the track! We must have a serious talk this minute!"

There is instant silence as the children respond to the note of near-hysteria in my voice. The boys are flushed and worried, unsure of what has gone wrong. I have asked them to do the impossible: separate running from fantasy without the structure of an organized game.

"Look, boys——"

"Andrew was chasing. Not me."

"It was Jonathan. I told him to stop."

"I was only running."

"Never mind, boys. Look, here's the problem. The track takes up too much space. It crowds the sandbox and record player too close together. We're going to have to take away the track."

If the boys are disappointed, it does not show. In fact, they seem relieved. The track has imposed a burden that neither they nor I can handle, but, as with most classroom events that misfire, we gain new perspectives on the obvious. The best insights appear, it seems, when the unexpected happens.

13

"When can we have our track again?" Charlotte asks, several days after the tape is gone. None of the boys has mentioned the track.

"There's no room for it, Charlotte. But, you know, we could use the high school track during their lunch period."

Charlotte rushes the news to everyone. "We're going to have a track meeting!" There is a great amount of excitement, and I have no choice but to rearrange our schedule so we can be outdoors at noon.

The high school athletic field is next to our playground. Sometimes the children and I watch track meets through the chain-link fence that separates the two areas. As soon as we get to the track, the boys stretch and crouch and begin to measure one another's speed. "I'm winning you!" someone shouts. They throw back their heads, squinting into the sun, and self-consciously lengthen their stride. There is no superhero play, no chasing, flying, or shooting. Another kind of superhero emerges—the athlete—but he will not stay long. It is too early for real contests of strength and endurance; magical heroes are more dependable. The boys keep up a track-star image for two days and then return to the playground, without a glance across the fence.

The girls ignore the heroic aspects of the sport. They run in twos and threes, slowing down so they can stay together and hold hands. Walking back, they speak of playing "house" and Snow White. Charlotte says the track is too big. She wishes we still had the little one in our room. Her nostalgia makes me curious about the sort of fantasies the girls created on our pretend track. Certainly the real track on which they had seen older girls run did not hold their interest. Unlike the boys, who immediately identified with grownup runners, the girls played "running" as they play "school" in the doll corner.

Charlotte, Mary Ann, Jill, and Karen are the four who counted laps, waiting each day until midmorning when the classroom track was cleared of boys. They called it the "girls' running school," and it would have attracted more girls had the track lasted longer. I feel guilty; the girls were deprived of exercise because the boys' fantasies got out of hand. Are the girls getting enough exercise? My image tends to be of girls sitting and boys running.

As I watch more carefully, what I see surprises me: The girls run more and the boys less than I thought. The total running time of the boys, of course, is greater, However, I consistently stop them sooner. Often they sound as if they are running when they are only shooting. My tolerance for running is directly related to what the runner is pretending and not to noise or distance covered.

Sisters chasing kittens, yelling and meowing, play out their scene and run back to the doll corner. Nor do I often interrupt ladies running in high heels, screaming with laughter. Skipping princesses arguing over a red velvet cape receive extra chasing time before arbitration is imposed.

However, the boy who runs out of the block area with a Tinker Toy gun in hand is stopped abruptly. He is not noisier than an escaping kitten, but he sounds more violent. He probably has less aggressive intent than the girls grabbing the red cape, but his fantasy makes me uneasy.

Teacher: The room is too noisy lately. I feel like closing the door so people don't hear us.
Mary Ann: The boys are noisy. Not us.
Teacher: You girls are noisy in the doll corner.
Mary Ann: They're much, much, much noisier.
Teacher: I'm not so sure.
Andrew: Boys have heavier shoes.
Paul: And stronger feet. That's what makes noise.

These illusions of power color our perceptions. When the indoor track became a focus for fantasy play, the girls left. Yet the boys are never rough with them; even on the playground, a girl is captured gently and only with her permission. The boys challenge one another, not the girls, but receive little credit for their good manners. A running boy is viewed with alarm unless he is part of an athletic team.

Fortunately, we have some form of organized running nearly every day, usually in room 214, a makeshift kindergarten gym. We play dodge ball and kick ball and have relay races and other running games, all directed by the teacher, a whistle, and unimpeachable rules. Each child is a proud member of Team A or Team B, but if the period extends beyond twenty or thirty minutes, another sort of play erupts: "Pretend you're a storm trooper and I see you coming. . . ." "And I'm the mother and you have to be the baby. . . ."

After the girls' reaction to the boys on the classroom track, I begin to wonder if they feel intimidated in games such as dodge ball, where the boys throw harder and behave more competitively.

"Do you remember when the girls wanted their own running club?" I ask one day.

"But you took away the track," Charlotte says.

"I know. But I'm thinking about room 214. Would it be fun if the girls went up sometimes without the boys?"

"Why can't *we* go up without the girls?" Jonathan asks.

"Okay. You can both do it."

The children cheer, as I knew they would. Whenever boys and girls are separated for an activity, there is a strong positive response on both sides. The new plan is easy to try out, since only half of the class can use room 214 at one time. Mrs. Brandt remains in the classroom with the boys, and I take the girls first.

It is soon clear that the dodge-ball game is in trouble. I expect the girls to perform more vigorously with no boys around to grab the ball, but instead they seem distracted. Two sit down in the way of the ball, and two others are talking about each other's dresses. I repeatedly call for attention. "Watch the ball, Janie!" "It's your turn, Mary Ann!" "Come on, girls, stand on the circle and throw harder." When our kick-ball game turns out to be equally spiritless, I put on a record. Suddenly every girl is on her toes skipping around in pairs.

"Oh, that was really fun!" Charlotte says to the boys as they line up for their turn. The boys are ready for their own brand of fun. There is a surge of competitiveness, signified by excessive quarreling and yelling: "He cheated!" "That's my ball!" Some throw the ball so hard I must keep reminding them to slow down and aim low. In every game, there is more physical contact and aggressive language than is customary. The boys look as if they are shooting one another with the ball. No wonder dodge ball and kick ball make sense to them; two years of aiming weapons and chasing bad guys have given the boys a significant head start in athletic exercises. After twenty minutes the boys are hot and sweaty. We switch to "A 'Tisket, a 'Tasket," and they relax immediately.

Back in the room, I ask the children how they think it went and everyone cheers.

"I don't agree," I tell them. "I think it's better when boys and girls are together."

"Why?" Charlotte asks, surprised.

"You play better and everyone acts nicer. However, let's try it one more day." More cheers.

The next day, there is the same inattentiveness from the girls and combativeness among the boys. I cite the incidents that prove my point, but no one is listening. They like the idea of separation as a matter of principle, not logic.

Later I ask, "How do you think 214 was today?"

"Great! Very terrific!"

"Perhaps so. But we can't continue the new plan."

"Why not?"

"Well, at this school, boys and girls have gym together."

"The high school doesn't," Charlotte remembers. "The boys and girls had different races."

"That's true. In some sports they do that. But not in Lower School."

I take the easy way out by invoking school policy. When we reassemble in room 214, boys and girls together, I see the balance more clearly. The boys quicken the pace and help the girls concentrate on the game, while the presence of the girls serves to mitigate the competitive fervor. Playing together makes the girls livelier and the boys more agreeable.

I must be careful: So eager are the boys and girls to have separate play worlds that I am almost fooled into believing they don't need each other.

14　　"Guess what Andrew did when you took the girls to 214," Mrs. Brandt says during our after-school coffee.

"I forgot to ask about that. What happened?"

"He and Jonathan played in the doll corner—ordinary doll-corner play. Jonathan said, 'Pretend I was just born,' and Andrew rocked him in the crib. Then, of course, they got silly."

"What did the other boys do?"

"Played in the blocks. Teddy played checkers with Jeremy. Teddy cheats, by the way."

"I wondered how he got so many kings. How about the girls? What did they do when the boys were upstairs?"

"Mostly they finger-painted. Charlotte made up a song and all the girls sang it while they painted. Something about a mushy wedding cake."

I am curious to see more. The next day I arrange for Mrs. Brandt to take the boys first and then the girls to the library. Again the girls congregate, this time in the blocks. They bring in armloads of blankets, dishes, clothes, and pillows and use nearly every block to build a six-room house filled with beds.

"This is the palace," Mary Ann says. "We're the Twelve Dancing Princesses." They drape themselves in shawls and scarves and run around scavenging items for the palace. Every few moments they return to lie down or rearrange the beds.

"Pretend we're asleep."

"Pretend we're in the forest."

"Pretend the princes can't find us because we're sleeping."

The absence of boys binds the girls together; they achieve a sense of community by sharing a particularly feminine activity. The painting table will do, but a fairy tale about twelve princesses who mysteriously wear out their shoes dancing every night is even better. The rest of the story doesn't matter; the girls rehearse the first part only. In their play the twelve sisters go on walking in the enchanted forest and live together forever.

When the boys return from the library, the girls dash for the beds.

"What are you doing?" Andrew asks.

"Sleeping," says Charlotte. "We're sound asleep. We're the dancing princesses."

"Oh." The boys disperse to other parts of the room, quieter than usual, and the girls remain inside the palace until clean-up time.

Later, when the girls go to the library, I expect the boys to resume the morning's interrupted space war in the blocks. Instead, they have a "work" period—no superheroes, running, or "messing around." The train tracks are laid out and garages, buildings, harbors, and airports begin to appear.

There is nothing exceptional about this engineering display. The boys spend more than half their block time "working," a fact I discovered while clocking indoor running habits. I would have guessed that seventy five percent of block play is devoted to superheroes, evidence perhaps that negative feelings affect my sense of time.

The nature of block play at any given time is determined by chance. A boy runs in saying "I'm Darth Vader" and the scene is set for Star Wars. Or, as happens today, the first boy to enter the blocks gets out the train tracks. Then an alternative kind of fantasy play, celebrating the mechanics of transportation and tall buildings, takes place.

Usually small groups of two or three boys work on separate constructions. However, as the number of projects or the number of boys in any one project increases, arguments multiply. Space is limited and there are a finite number of blocks and accessories. One of three things then occurs: The boys settle the quarrels and connect their buildings; the teacher arbitrates; or the boys, sensing they've had enough "work," switch to a superhero format in order to revive group spirit.

Superheroes, I am starting to realize, don't argue as much as "workmen." Perhaps when you pretend to fight, you don't really need to fight. Or maybe a superhero does not need to prove he is powerful; his label tells the story. A builder, confronted by a collapsed block structure, has no such sustaining symbol of competence.

The girls are more affected by the absence of the opposite

sex than are the boys. Though the boys were more aggressive in room 214 and less so in the classroom, they stayed in character. From Batman to dodge ball is an easy transaction. The boys are used to teams, whether of superheroes or city builders.

Teaming up is not commonplace among the girls; being alone in the classroom had the same effect as nail polishing: heightened group consciousness. Perhaps for this reason, a day later the girls are reminded of certain sexual inequities.

> Charlotte: The boys still use up all the blocks, even though we moved the doll corner.
> Mary Ann: Why can't we be alone today?
> Teacher: We can't do that all the time. Maybe once in a while.
> Janie: They don't take turns.
> Andrew: We never say they can't come in. I never did that.
> Teacher: I know. Look, you girls always start off at the tables. That's why the boys use up the blocks.
> Mary Ann: Let them go to the tables first!
> Jonathan: I don't want to!
> Teddy: Maybe the girls don't want to come in because it's too crowded.
> Paul: Maybe the girls don't want to play in the blocks because they're playing with their dolls.
> Charlotte: I *want* to go in the blocks. But it seems like it's all tooken up and it's filled with boys.
> Clarice: The boys could have a little time of it and they could let somebody else have the blocks.
> Andrew: But maybe we're not finished. Maybe we just started something new.
> Paul: It takes too long to build. Then there's no time to play in it.
> Teacher: This is a hard problem. Nobody keeps the girls out, but they like to do other things first.
> Charlotte: All right. I'll go in there as soon as I come.
> Mary Ann: Me too.
> Karen: Me too.

The next day I remind the girls of their decision to start off in the blocks, and four of them begin to build a house immediately. They play as they would in the doll corner—mother, two sisters, and a baby—except they must build the environment before playing in it.

On subsequent mornings the girls resume their habit of going directly to the art tables. By the time they finish painting and drawing, the block area is full of spaceships. There are no regretful murmurs about boys monopolizing blocks, however. Apparently the girls no longer feel victimized. The invisible curtain descends around the doll corner as they disappear into old bed jackets, frilly blouses, floppy hats, and high heels. When Charlotte emerges she has a new story to dictate, a romantic tale that requires the participation of two male characters. Unlike superheroes, the dancing princesses do not remain forever alone:

> Once upon a time there was six beautiful
> princesses, but two was the most beautiful and the
> others just was a little bit beautiful. They danced all
> night long and in the morning their shoes were all
> worn out. Two was not worn out. Then two princes
> came and married the two princesses. But they didn't
> live in the same castle. They lived in two different
> separate castles and one had gold in it.

15 The juxtaposition of the doll-corner boudoir and the spaceship next door brings to mind an old concern: Are the girls missing an important experience? Not superhero play—the girls have their own. Mothers and princesses are as powerful as any superheroes the boys can devise. I refer to the building activities themselves. The physical energy and mathematical calculations that go into block construction are not necessary in the doll corner, where the stage setting is always ready and waiting.

It is quite another thing when the girls set up housekeeping in the block area. Half of the time is spent comparing, estimating, and organizing graded materials: heavy hollow blocks for walls, long narrow ones for the floor, various combinations of both for tables, chairs and beds. The work involved seems to imbue the play with a unified theme. Because they are so aware of every aspect of an environment they have themselves built, the girls are less inclined to become distracted.

In kindergarten the girl who builds regularly is a rarity, while most boys build something every day. For girls, block play has become an afterthought, enjoyed as a novelty but forgotten when the daily agenda is planned. This is not the case in nursery school, where many girls spend as much time in the blocks as the boys. Charlotte and Mary Ann had the reputation of being master builders and were often asked for help by the younger boys and girls. Charlotte, for a while, called herself a "house builder." This was at a time when her stories had male heroes and giant bears. Now that Charlotte is in kindergarten, her stories are about princesses and she builds only occasionally. She says she is too busy "making presents" and, besides, the block area is "tooken up with boys."

Deficiencies in block building seem to hold no immediate consequences for the girls; but, to me, the boys carry the image of future engineers and the girls seem deprived. As for the building skills themselves, comparisons are hard to make. Boys and girls build different structures. Their dwellings answer to the needs of particular dramatic themes: bungalows for girls and spaceships for boys. However, in addition to dramatic props, the boys construct buildings for the sheer pleasure of putting pieces together in new ways and making structures grow large. There are complex designs that depend on a precise balance between dozens of small blocks and symmetrical patterns using curved blocks and arches. The girls have not practiced these forms; they do not display the same kind of structural imagery with blocks as they do with crayons on paper.

I like to watch the boys' buildings going up, but I am not satisfied that the builder's vision is theirs alone. Car play is even more exclusively male, yet I do not urge the girls to take an interest, especially now when stunt driving has become a daily event. Could the girls possibly enjoy building a house next to a fleet of tiny cars that continuously jump over collapsing bridges? Perhaps, I reason, if the girls had a more private place to build, their affection for blocks would return.

> Teacher: The other day I watched you girls building a house. Wouldn't it be fun to build your own house every day instead of having a doll corner that's already made?
>
> Mary Ann: The doll corner is builded. The walls are there.
>
> Teacher: But what if we kept a supply of blocks in the doll corner? Then you could build things just the way you want them, and the boys wouldn't use up all the blocks before you got there.
>
> Charlotte: You can't build a doll corner, or the walls will fall down. Even the school could fall down.
>
> Teacher: But why can't you build a house inside the doll corner? The boys build ships inside the block corner.
>
> Karen: Because they already have a block corner.
>
> Teacher: Anyone can use that space.
>
> Charlotte: But a doll corner always has to be a doll corner.
>
> Teacher: How about when the boys play Star Wars in the doll corner?
>
> Charlotte: They just pretend it's Star Wars.
>
> Teacher: But in the block area it's *really* Star Wars?
>
> Charlotte: Yeah. But we could make a house there if we want.
>
> Teacher: What if there were no boys in this class? What would happen to the block corner?
>
> Charlotte: You could call it a girls' block corner.

My approach is too abstract. I am asking the girls to imagine a different form for a space they take for granted. I switch to a more direct course:

Teacher: Actually, this is what I have in mind. I'd
    like to see what the doll corner is like without
    ready-made furniture. If we put all the furniture in
    Mr. Pickens's closet for a few days and bring up
    the old blocks that are in the basement, we can see
    what happens. We'll keep the clothes, blankets,
    dishes, dolls, and pillows, but you can build
    everything else.
Karen: Then can we have it back?
Teacher: Absolutely. This is just an experiment, like
    when you moved the doll corner closer to the
    blocks. Now the doll corner will have its own
    blocks.

The girls nod in hesitant agreement, but the boys are wildly
enthusiastic. This is the sort of "work job" they love. We move
the furniture into the hall and begin the long trek to the basement where the forty-year-old dark-stained blocks are stored.
Block by block, in assembly-line manner, we transfer the supply to our room.

The blocks are in worse condition than I remembered.
"We'll have to sand these blocks before we can use them.
They're a bit splintery." The children don't mind. At this point
everything seems like a game. The procession has become a
festive event with spontaneous singing that causes several
nearby classrooms to close their doors.

The sanded blocks are to be stacked against the doll-corner
walls, but before I know it, the boys have begun to build a
tower outside the doll corner. Andrew stands on a chair while
Jeremy hands him the freshly sanded blocks. The tower is already above Andrew's head.

The girls, on the other hand, lose interest the moment they
stop sanding. Charlotte and Mary Ann are swinging on the
climbing ladder, Karen and Clarice have spread newspapers
on the floor in preparation for splatter painting, and several
other girls are cutting and folding colored tissue paper. None
of the girls pays any attention to the basement blocks.

Not surprisingly, the experiment backfires. The girls set up two new doll corners, one under the climbing ladder and the other in the cubby room. Blankets are draped along the horizontal bars to create walls around the gym mats below, and the cubby-room floor disappears under layers of little rugs. Dolls, clothes, and dishes lie in messy heaps, an obstacle to good play, it seems to me, but the girls prefer their inventions to mine.

The boys ignore the makeshift doll corners; it is the blocks they covet. "Can we use the new blocks? The girls don't want them!"

"Ask them. See if they intend to use them."

The girls insist they need the blocks. "Don't touch them!" Charlotte warns. At dismissal time the blocks have still not been used.

The next day the boys drive trucks into the empty doll corner and call it a parking lot. They bring in enough of the regular block supply to make a multilevel garage. My pilot program has gotten out of hand. The abandoned doll corner is about to be swallowed up, the cubby room is virtually impassable, and there are girls sitting on the ladder, under a blanket, chanting, "Boys, boys, stop the noise."

On the third day of the experiment, half of the girls do not even come out of the cubby room after they hang up their coats. Any boy who enters is screamed at: "Get out! Private property!"

"Wait a moment, girls," I say. "This really won't do. We must have a talk. The doll-corner experiment is not working."

"Why not?"

"Well, look. Nobody is using the basement blocks to make the house and furniture. That was the whole point."

The girls stare at the doll corner and then look around the room. None of us has anything to say, as if we are not quite sure what subject is being discussed. The blocks appear void of image or purpose. Apparently the doll corner can be brought into the blocks, but the blocks cannot be brought into the doll corner.

"Can't we play in the cubby room?" Clarice asks.

"Not really. People just can't get their coats, you know."

There is a long pause. Clarice gets up and walks around. "Could we have the doll corner again and the furniture, too?"

"That's a good idea. Let's ask Mr. Pickens to bring back the furniture." My relief is as obvious as the girls'.

Andrew and Paul come running up. "Can we have the new blocks? We really need them."

"They could use them for a while," Charlotte says.

The boys perform their newest ritual—the assembly line—to move the blocks. Cleanup time takes twice as long this way, but the boys like the looks of it. The girls deliberately avoid the old blocks and become overly fastidious as they fold doll clothing and line up pairs of shoes to fit into each space that opens up as a row of blocks is removed.

My attempt to manipulate their fantasy play seems to have no lasting effect on the girls. We retrieve the furniture ourselves the following day. I borrow the custodian's dolly and, in less than an hour, the table, stove, refrigerator, cribs, and dressers are back in place. With an unerring instinct for group ceremonies, the girls spend afternoon playtime taping colored tissue paper all over the doll corner.

16   "Pretend these are bricks," says Mary Ann. "This is the pigs' house." She and Charlotte no longer ignore the basement blocks now that they are piled up in the block corner, where they belong.

"Not the one with the wolf," Charlotte cautions. "A different one."

"Don't make a chimney."

The old-fashioned blocks do resemble bricks, being smaller yet heavier than the modern variety. The connection to "The

Three Pigs" is made when the class returns from hearing the story in the library.

"I'm Cinderella," Charlotte decides. "You be Snow White." She and Mary Ann will be sisters who live in a brick house with no chimney, in a woods that has no wolf. "Pretend our mother is poor and we got lost and then we see a brick house that's empty."

"But really a godmother lives there——"

"And she's taking a walk and then she sees the two little girls and she's not angry."

At the far side of the block area, Andrew and Paul have crawled inside a large cardboard carton that had been a spaceship but is now a chimney.

"Pretend you're Wolfman and you come down the chimney and boil the wolf," Andrew says. "And the next day the wolf jumps down the chimney and I'm Superman and I explode him. First I jump over him."

"No, the wolf throws a brick at Superman and it bounces right off and he flies up. . . ."

The boys seldom bring fairy tales into their play; but the librarian's story is still on everyone's mind. She told the original story, in which the first two pigs are eaten by the wolf; the children are more familiar with the modern version, which allows all three pigs to escape unharmed. The serene brick house on one side of the room and the turbulent chimney on the other seem to imply that boys and girls find a different meaning in the story. However, as we talk about the story, everyone's main concern becomes the little pigs' separation from their mother.

> Teacher: I wonder why the three pigs decide to build
>   separate houses.
> Clarice: They didn't have enough room and they
>   needed a small house because they were all small.
> Andrew: They wouldn't have enough food.
> Jeremy: They wanted to live by theirselves so they
>   could have their own stuff.

Charlotte: They want to live alone.

Paul: They needed to be separate so they wouldn't be so sad about not living with their mother.

Andrew: Some would be near and some would be far from the mother.

Robert: They should build houses far away from each other so they wouldn't fight, or they would worry about the third pig getting all the apples.

Mary Ann: Sometimes pigs do fight about things.

Paul: Maybe they think they will live with their mother. One of them will, and not the others in the other houses. Then if the wolf blows the house down, one could run home.

Jill: The pigs are so little they might be able to run very slow.

Paul: They don't have to go in the woods. They could stay home.

Charlotte: No. The mother is old and she wants to live by herself.

Ned: Because she didn't have even enough money.

Clarice: They might get lost when she went to the bank to buy the money.

Ned: When she went to the bank they could have stayed home.

Teacher: Did she know that a wolf lived in the woods?

Charlotte: Oh, no! She didn't know that.

Ned: She thought he was already boiled. The father told her.

Teacher: Is there a father?

Jill: Maybe he was at work.

Charlotte: Maybe the father pig gotten eaten by the wolf.

Ned: Maybe he got killed.

Andrew: What Charlotte said I don't think is true, because then the mother pig would know that the wolf lived in the forest.

Mary Ann: The pigs could of told her. They would be out with the father. Why wouldn't the wolf have ate them if they were out with the father? So he couldn't have gotten ate.

Paul: Maybe their dad got lost. Or maybe a tree fell on him.

Karen: Wait—I know! Maybe a tree got loose and the father was under a tree that was loose and the wolf was behind the tree and the wolf pushed it down.

Jonathan: Then he fell down and the wolf ate him, but the mother doesn't know.

Mary Ann: She didn't know wolves can blow down houses.

Jeremy: If she knew, she wouldn't let her children out.

Charlotte: She thought they would all make brick houses.

Andrew: The wolf could come back and blow down the house.

Charlotte: No, he can't. They all live happily ever after.

Teddy: Wolves are much stronger than pigs, but a pig can trick a wolf.

Paul: I think they've got to go home because there's something important they have to watch. Out in the woods is a big bad wolf.

Karen: In my book all the pigs run away and he doesn't eat them.

Teacher: Who likes that better?

Everyone prefers the safer version. Paul wants the pigs to be safe, yet he offers them no protection in his story:

There was three pigs, and a giant monster wolf huffed and puffed on them and they were dead. Then a dragon blowed fire on the wolf and he got boiled.

Poor Paul. Since he cannot include a mother in his story or deny the existence of the wolf, he must become a dragon more powerful than the wolf.

Mary Ann also wants all three pigs to escape unharmed, and her story provides an easy solution:

There was three pigs and their mother said, "Don't
go in the woods. There is a wolf." So the pigs had a
picnic, but not in the woods. Then the mother said,
"I forgot. There isn't not a wolf."

No wonder the boys carry on so fiercely. They identify with
the little pigs as certainly as do the girls, but they must pretend they don't care about little pigs or their mothers when
they play. The more unprotected the boys feel, the louder they
roar.

In the afternoon we perform "The Three Pigs," and eight
boys want to be the wolf.

"Why do you boys want so much to be the wolf?" I ask. "He
does end up getting cooked."

"But he's stronger," Andrew says. "He's got sharp teeth. And
he can jump on the roof."

"And blow the wind," adds Paul.

"The pig is smarter," says Mary Ann.

"He *is* smarter"—Andrew nods—"but not stronger."

"The pig could be strong," says Jonathan, who has agreed to
be the pig. "Wait a minute. I have to get something from my
cubby." He brings back the Star Wars light saber he made
earlier in the day.

Charlotte disapproves. "The pig can't have that."

"Sure he can," Jonathan tells her. "If the wolf jumps over
the boiling water, I cut off his head."

Charlotte, the mother pig, shakes her head. "Bring the
mother, Jonathan. She'll be better at boiling things."

Teddy does not want to be in the play. Nor does he have
much to say during the discussion. But he dictates a story that
wins every boy's approval:

Superman, Batman, Spiderman, and
Wonderwoman went into the woods and they went
into the house where the pigs lived. They saw a
wicked witch. She gave them poisoned food. Then
they died. Then Wonderwoman had magic and they
woke up. Everybody didn't wake up. Then they woke

up from Wonderwoman's magic. They saw a
chimney and the wolf opened his mouth. Superman
exploded him.

Teddy laughs out loud. It is his first Superman story and the
first story in which he has given himself the strongest role.

17   I am "hooked" on fairy-tale talk. The follow-
     ing week I read "The Three Bears" and try to
     find out how the children feel about Goldi-
     locks.

Teacher: What sort of girl is Goldilocks?
Andrew: She's curious.
Teacher: What does "curious" mean?
Andrew: That you get into trouble.
Charlotte: She's a robber. She eats food and goes into
    houses.
Mary Ann: That's right. She could be a robber.
    Robbers go into people's houses.
Teacher: Did she plan on robbing the bears?
Jill: Yes she did. They forgot to lock the door. The
    father said, "Don't forget to lock the door."
Janie: She *is* a robber. She could of stoled their
    money.
Teddy: Maybe her parents got killed and she was
    looking for a house.
Franklin: She just wanted to go in the house. She
    wanted to sit in a chair because she was tired from
    walking too much.
Teacher: Why was she in the woods?
Jonathan: Probably she got lost and she was looking
    for a new house.
Jill: Or looking for blackberries.
Charlotte: Maybe she was coming home from school
    and she was looking for her house and she found
    that house.

Mary Ann: Maybe she was looking for blackberries and she thought this was the way she always went through the woods, but it wasn't.

Teddy: Maybe she was cutting down wood.

Clarice: What if she thinks it's her own house?

Charlotte: She *did* think it's her own house. She probably has the same furniture.

Karen: That could happen.

Jeremy: She went in because of being tired. And when she heard footprints she thought it was her mommy and father. And when she woke up it was the bears.

Jill: She dreamed that they would hurt her.

Andrew: She thought they'll cut her up and use her for their next porridge.

Mary Ann: They might or they might not.

Andrew: Bears always do.

Goldilocks's image changes quickly. First she is a trouble-seeking invader and then, suddenly, she is a lost child at the mercy of a family of bears.

The boys throughout have been sympathetic to Goldilocks; it is their insistence that she is lost that wins the girls away from the robber theory. The next day Charlotte makes a Goldilocks puppet and brings it to the circle at piano time. I say:

"Charlotte's puppet reminds me of something I meant to ask yesterday. How would you feel if Goldilocks came to your house to play?"

Charlotte quickly welcomes the prospect. The next eight respondents are girls—it is the girls' side—and they all agree with Charlotte. The first boys on the circle, Ned and Teddy, also nod their approval.

Andrew can barely wait for his turn. "No way!" he yells. The boys jump in response. Paul and Jeremy laugh loudly. "She better not! Oh, no!"

Ned waves his arms. "I changed my mind!"

"Why?" I ask.

"Because she'll play with the games I hate."

Franklin is next. "Uh-uh!" One after another now the boys treat my question with disdain.

"Never in infinity!"

"No way, no way!"

"If she comes, shoot her up to the moon!"

"Blast her to Jupiter!"

"Okay," I venture, "the girls like the idea and the boys don't."

Teddy objects: "I still do. I didn't change my mind."

"Can you tell us why?"

"Because Goldilocks doesn't like bears and I don't also."

There is respectful silence. Teddy has not joined the boys in their exaggerated display of chauvinism and his position is acceptable. The boys would, I think, all like to play with Goldilocks, but my decision to question the children one by one around the circle focused on its division by sex and created a boy-girl issue.

The girls may also have been seized by a touch of chauvinism. They say they are eager to play with Goldilocks, but, in fact, they never "play" with her in the doll corner. That is, no one says "I'm Goldilocks," as they always say "I'm Snow White." They pretend they are either ordinary sisters in household dramas that have no wolves, bears, or witches, or else they are princesses—Snow White, Cinderella, Sleeping Beauty—who are protected by magic.

Just as the three pigs seem too fragile, Goldilocks is at the mercy of the bears. Neither she nor the bears arouse feelings of loyalty. Goldilocks is not safe enough for the girls, and the bears lack the dangerous quality that might endear them to the boys. Andrew, however, has an idea that, for the moment, resolves his ambivalent feelings about Goldilocks:

> Once there was Goldilocks, and she didn't live with
> the bears, she lived by herself. And one day
> Goldilocks came and the bears saw her. And they
> knew it was time for throwing her into the dungeon.
> They wanted to have a feast. They ate her.

Clarice deals with Goldilocks in a different way. She tells this story, taking for herself the role of Cinderella and depriving Goldilocks of a picnic and friends:

> Goldilocks doesn't see the bears because she is sleeping. They decided to have a picnic, so they went to have a picnic under the old oak tree and they invited Cinderella to come. Goldilocks had to go home by herself. And their mother wasn't home.

After both stories are acted out, I ask if Goldilocks has any sisters or brothers. At first everyone says no, but a quick reconsideration results in a new consensus: Goldilocks has one brother and one sister, both of whom don't like her because she goes for walks in the woods.

"Why doesn't Goldilocks have a fairy godmother?" Clarice asks. "Like Cinderella."

"Would you like her better if she did?"

"Much better."

Clarice pinpoints the major obstacle in "The Three Bears" and "The Three Pigs": the absence of magic. The cleverness of the third pig is not dependable enough. He is perceived as a child and therefore would be too worried about his mother and his siblings to defend himself. As Andrew is quick to observe, "The wolf could come back and blow down the house."

As for Goldilocks, she lacks all visible support, except perhaps the dubious ability to outrun the bears. If she is alone, to whom will she run? If she has a family, why don't they care about her? Lacking parents or siblings who protect her, she needs a fairy godmother or at least glass slippers.

When we act out "The Three Bears," nearly all the children want to be Baby Bear. He is well cared for by his parents, who walk with him in the woods; there is never a threat that he will be abandoned or harmed. Charlotte captures the feeling in her Baby Bear story:

> Baby Bear said, "Someone's been sleeping in my

bed." Then they all went on a boat. Then they had a picnic and they had a party.

18 The children make changes in all the fairy tales now, though they want me to read the original version. Charlotte will be the smallest pig if all three pigs live together, without a chimney. Jonathan wants a chimney but a better armed pig. His light saber is more dependable than a pot of boiling water. As always, the girls eliminate the violence, and the boys seek a stronger hero.

I am beginning to wonder if we might be better off just listening to fairy tales and talking about them but not acting them out. It matters almost too much to children which role they take, as though the commitment might outlast the story. Moreover, the plot is often severely curtailed. For example, in his version of "Jack and the Beanstalk," Paul dispenses with the giant quickly, and avoids the chase scene down the beanstalk.

Jack heard "Fee, fie, fo, fum!" Then the giant came in. Then Jack gave the giant some poison, and he was dead.

Either Paul is too impatient to go through the steps required to defeat the giant or he doesn't trust the outcome. Giants and wolves are dangerous, and heroes are easily tricked.

When I tell "Little Red Riding Hood," suspense hovers over each turn in the plot. As Red Riding Hood comes face to face with the wolf for the first time, Paul asks, "Is there going to be a woodcutter?" Paul has heard the story dozens of times, yet he still wants to know if the woodcutter will appear.

Later in the story, an unintentional error of mine causes some anxious responses. Misquoting Red Riding Hood's exact words to the wolf, instead of "nose" I say, "Grandmother, what big *arms* you have!" Janie looks startled and whispers, "The better to hug you with." Greg doesn't even give me a chance to finish my "Grandmother, what big teeth you have!" before he says, "The better to lick you with." Whereupon Jill warns, "Don't look at people who look like wolves." Her comment puzzles me and later I ask:

> Teacher: Jill, what did you mean when you said, "Don't look at people who look like wolves"?
> Jill: Her mother said it to her. She didn't know it's a wolf.
> Teacher: Who does Red Riding Hood think it is?
> Jill: Just a person who doesn't look exactly like other people.
> Mary Ann: Maybe she thinks it's a dog.
> Franklin: She just thinks it's a friendly wolf.
> Teacher: Shouldn't she have been suspicious? Are wolves supposed to be friendly?
> Charlotte: Maybe she only believed that wolves who are nice they are very, very good.
> Mary Ann: She believed in friendly wolves.
> Andrew: She thought he was a friendly fox.
> Charlotte: No. She knew it was a wolf, but she thought he was a friendly wolf and she forgot what her mother said.
> Jill: Maybe she thought it was a person in a fur coat.
> Robert: Or a dog.
> Ned: Maybe a person in a costume.
> Teddy: If the sun was in her eyes, she couldn't tell it was a costume.

The children downplay the threat of the wolf and find excuses for Red Riding Hood's gullibility. That one can be so easily fooled by a wolf is a worrisome notion.

> Teacher: How can Red Riding Hood really believe that the wolf is her grandmother?
> Charlotte: He says "Hi" just like her grandmother does, so that fools her.

Jill: She thought her grandmother's face changed because she was sick.

Clarice: Probably if she had a face full of bumps, she might have thought she had chicken pox.

Andrew: Maybe she thought she changed into a wolf by a witch.

Paul: Maybe she knew it was the wolf and she knew he ate her grandmother and she was tricking him.

Andrew: You mean she wanted to meet her grandmother in the wolf's stomach?

Charlotte: She knew somebody would soon come out and cut her open.

Andrew: She must of saw the woodcutter in the forest. And he had an ax.

Teddy: Probably she saw her dad from a long distance. And *he* had an ax.

Andrew: Maybe *she* had an ax.

Teddy: She could cut off his head.

Charlotte: No. It has to be the woodcutter. She's just a little girl.

Teacher: What if Red Riding Hood was a little boy?

Charlotte: Maybe a little boy could do it, because he could pretend to be a woodcutter.

Teddy: He could pretend to be a werewolf.

19   The girls are in room 214 with Mrs. Brandt as the boys and I prepare to talk about "Jack and the Beanstalk." They are seated on the circle, self-conscious and impatient. In the few moments it takes me to rewind the tape recorder, Andrew tears Jonathan's picture, Paul tosses Greg's Darth Vader figure into the air, and Jeremy sits on Teddy's finger.

Andrew answers my first question irreverently, and the others copy him. However, when we speak of Jack's mother or the giant's wife, the boys become serious. Throughout the discussion, they swing back and forth between sincerity and burlesque as if continually putting on a mask and taking it off.

Teacher: Why does Jack take a chance climbing up the beanstalk when he doesn't know where it goes?

Jonathan: He thinks it goes to heaven.

Andrew: You must mean to the moon. (He laughs, and the others giggle and wave their arms.)

Paul: It goes to Mars. He jumps all over Mars. (Laughter)

Teddy: Maybe he thinks there's some kind of treasure.

Jeremy: Maybe he just wants to see what's up there.

Jacob: He's going to zoomerang to Jupiter. (Laughter)

Robert: He'll blast off a hundred miles into space. Maybe his head will come off. (Laughter)

Andrew: Maybe he thought he'll see all those movies about Martians way up to Chicago so his skin could hang out. (Laughter)

Teacher: Why does the giant's wife help Jack?

Paul: She's not an ogre. She's a nice lady.

Andrew: Because he's nice. She thinks Jack is nice.

Greg: She doesn't want the giant to eat the boy.

Jeremy: She's worried that the giant eats boys.

Franklin: She wants a kid.

Teacher: Does she have children of her own?

Andrew: The giant might have growed up to be a giant. He used to be her child.

Teacher: Why does Jack go back after he steals the hen? After all, now he and his mother are no longer poor.

Andrew: Maybe he wants the giant to take him to the moon. (Laughter)

Jonathan: He wants the giant to eat him and eat the moon. (Laughter)

Paul: Maybe he wants to fall off the moon and kill himself. (Laughter)

Is it the story of Jack or the effect of an all-male group that causes this disruptive bravado? Jack is the one hero in all our fairy tales who most resembles the boys themselves. He leaves his mother and competes with a giant, outwitting but not becoming more powerful than the giant. Each time a question concerns Jack's climb up the beanstalk, the boys lapse into a stir-crazy act that prevents further consideration of the issue.

When it is the boys' turn to go upstairs, the girls take their places on the circle. The contrast between the two groups is startling. I relax instantly, confident that the girls will sit quietly and pay attention.

Teacher: Why does Jack decide to climb the beanstalk?

Charlotte: He wants to find out what was up there.

Mary Ann: Maybe he thinks it's very cloudy up there and he doesn't know if there's a king or a giant there, so he just wants to know.

Clarice: He wants to find out if there's a house up there to rest.

Jill: Maybe he thinks they're rich up there and there's lots of food.

Teacher: Why does the giant's wife help Jack?

Karen: She likes little boys. She doesn't want the giant to eat him.

Janice: She's the good one and the giant is the bad guy.

Charlotte: Maybe she doesn't want her husband to get fat. (All the girls smile at this single attempt at levity during their discussion.)

Teacher: Does she have children of her own?

Janice: Maybe she had a little boy and he grew taller and taller and he was very old.

Charlotte: He grew up to be the giant.

Teacher: Why does Jack go back after he steals the hen?

Mary Ann: Maybe he didn't steal it. Maybe she said, "Here, take it. You'll get very rich from the golden eggs." So he knows she'll give him more good stuff.

Clarice: He knows the queen will hide him in the oven. She likes him. She's lonely, too.

Jill: He thinks the queen will give him a harp.

Mary Ann: You mean give him something. He doesn't know about the harp.

Jill: Yeah. I mean a treasure.

Teacher: Does Jack's mother know he's going back up there?

Everyone: No.

Mary Ann: She's sleeping. She thinks he's in bed. It's too early.

Charlotte: Maybe she thinks there's a very nice queen up there. She doesn't know about the giant.

When the boys return from room 214, it is time to go home. Andrew comes directly to me before getting his coat:

"You didn't ask if Jack goes back to see the giant's wife."

"Does he?"

"Yes. Because she might be his mother."

"Instead of his own mother?"

"He might want two mothers—one for the ground and one for the sky."

20 The boys cannot resist a giant any more than Jack can. At our Chinese New Year parade they conquer a fourteen-foot dragon, one of a pair outlined the day before by Franklin. The children want an even larger dragon, long enough for the whole class to carry, but I veto the idea.

"It will be too hard to stay in a single line," I insist. "Two smaller dragons are better."

The morning of the parade, Andrew and Jeremy arrive early and begin to color in one of the dragons. Then Charlotte walks in, glances briefly at what the boys are doing, and runs to the second dragon. Not told which dragon to color, the boys straddle the first dragon while the girls head for its mate. Thirty minutes later we have a male and a female dragon, one ablaze with Star Wars symbols and the other with a dainty flower garden.

The boys take on their dragon's coloration. Red flashes and

exploding rockets follow dotted lines until the dragon seems to breathe fire from every jagged point. It shifts and humps along the floor as the boys collide and enter one another's territory, sounding warning cries. Mrs. Brandt and I scurry back and forth uttering words of caution and applying masking tape to twelve boys and an embattled dragon.

A few feet away, the girls murmur over their brightly petaled flowers. "This is where the godmother stays," Charlotte says, putting Cinderella under a rainbow halo. Soon there are six more Cinderellas surrounded by rainbows and tulips. "Can we paste on tissue flowers?" "Can I use the doilies?" "I'm making valentines."

The boys observe the lady dragon with considerable interest, then plunge back into battle. "Pretend this dragon sees another dragon——"

"Your dragon is done, boys," I say quickly. "I'll put it away until the parade."

Once the dragon is out of sight, the boys go off to other activities, but their play reveals that the dragon has stirred up more excitement than can be channeled into drawings. Mrs. Brandt and I have an attack of second guessing: We shouldn't have made two dragons; the dragons ought to have been painted red all over; we should have organized boy-girl artist teams. Any of these choices might have produced a calmer dragon. Or perhaps not.

In any case, the parade lies ahead. In hopes of rehabilitating the dragon, I read a story brought to school by Karen, who is Chinese. It is about well-behaved Chinese children and smiling, gentle dragons.

"Here's a good idea," I say. "Let's have each dragon carried by boys and girls together. Just like this picture in the book."

The children stare at me in astonishment. They have purposely made a boy and a girl dragon. Would a boy wear a Cinderella costume on Halloween or a girl dress up as Darth Vader?

"Okay. I see you don't care for the idea. Then I must insist that everyone walk very, very slowly. No bumping or touching. No roaring."

The parade route is the long corridor between our room and another kindergarten class. Our plan seems simple. The boys and girls are to walk in adjacent rows, holding the two dragons as if they are opposite sides of one animal, boys on the right, girls on the left. In theory, the dragon will move quietly down the hallway; however, before we reach the first intersection, the boys' dragon rips apart. I send Jonathan back for the mending tape, and by the time he returns, the dragon has been torn twice more. The girls' side barely flutters as the disfigured dragon keeps lurching and groaning on its right side.

Mrs. Brandt and I perform quick surgery on the dragon, whispering directions. "Come on, boys, people are watching. Walk calmly. Stop growling. Breathe deeply."

The more I glare at the boys the less coordinated they become. Heads, arms, and legs are thrust in all directions, jerking and ducking into the dragon, which continues to tear. People along the route cannot help laughing as the boys increase their manic behavior.

Mrs. Brandt and I hurriedly confer. We have two choices: send the boys back in disgrace or ignore them. One look at them, however, shows they do not realize they are in disgrace, so we decide to act as if nothing unusual is going on.

The march through the other kindergarten room is brief. "Your dragon is torn," a girl tells us. "On one side," I reply. We rush through a Chinese song that repeats "Good Luck, Happy New Year" three times and we return to our class. The boys race through the hall waving pieces of the dragon, but Mrs. Brandt and I walk along slowly with the girls, saying nothing.

In the room, the boys have already started to build with blocks. The dragon lies in a heap on the table.

"What did you think of the parade, boys?" I ask.

"Great!"

"Wonderful!"

"We had a great dragon!"

The boys mutilated their dragon and disrupted the parade, yet seem unaware that anything is wrong.

I turn to the girls: "How did you like the parade?"

"Wonderful!"

"We got two compliments."

"Can we have another parade?"

No one mentions the boys' behavior. Either the girls didn't notice the chaos or else they expect boy dragons to be wild.

"You said we could tape our dragon to the wall," Charlotte says.

"You can. But what about the boys' dragon?"

I put both dragons in the middle of the circle and call everyone to sit down.

> Teacher: The girls want to hang up their dragon.
> Andrew: Ours too.
> Teacher: That's what I want to talk about. Yours is torn.
> Paul: Who did it?
> Teacher: You boys did it.
> Jonathan: It only got torn two times. 'Member when I got the tape?
> Teacher: But no one else touched your dragon. Only you boys.
> Jeremy: The other side didn't get torn.
> Teacher: The other side walked slowly.
> Franklin: We was too walkin' slow.
> Andrew: Someone came and tore it up.
> Teacher: Who? When?
> Charlotte: Maybe some kid that doesn't like dragons.
> Mary Ann: Some kid that fights with them in the playground.

An hour after the parade, Mrs. Brandt takes the children to music class. The boys push and bump in the line and there are complaints all around.

"Stand quietly, boys," Mrs. Brandt says. "You act as if you're still holding the dragon." She walks them to the music room, and when she returns, Andrew is with her.

"I stayed to watch for a few minutes," she explains. "All the boys were getting yelled at, but Andrew was the worst, so I thought I'd better bring him back."

"What's wrong, Andrew? Are you still excited because of the dragon?"

"I don't feel excited," Andrew says. "I'm just tired."

"Do you want to rest on your rug?"

"Could I tape the dragon together, so it can hang on the wall like the girls'?"

I give him the tape and he spreads out the dragon like the pieces of a puzzle. His hands are calm and steady and he spends the next twenty minutes matching and taping pieces of dragon. After lunch he continues to make repairs, and a number of boys join him. By the end of the day a smaller, heavily taped dragon goes up on the wall beside its floral counterpart. There is no further active involvement in the dragon. It joins the giant pumpkin, the Mayflower, Santa Claus, and other mementos of happy celebrations.

I decide not to lecture on the events of the parade—or of the music class, for that matter. The girls remained calm because their fantasies placed them in an enchanted garden, for which they received compliments plus the added bonus of an undamaged dragon. The boys took the dragon as seriously as Jack would have. They confronted it, tricked it, and destroyed it. It is the teacher who does not take dragons seriously, who prefers and expects dragons—and heroes—to remain inside the fairy-tale book.

21   The dragon incident reinforces the most commonly held classroom assumption: boys are more restless and disruptive than girls. While there are girls who get into trouble and boys who do not, in any class the boys will be significantly ahead when misdemeanors are counted.

The means by which offenses are tallied, explained, and managed vary widely, but there is general agreement that boys create more tension in a classroom than girls and that it has somehow to do with physical momentum. Webster's definition of momentum—"a property of a moving body that determines the length of time required to bring it to rest when under the action of a constant force"—seems custom-made for boys. Their unique combination of motion and aggressive fantasy is the "constant force," and the time required to bring them "to rest" is the problem in the classroom.

Momentum is an issue from the first day of school. The youngest boys in our building, the three-year-olds, are immediately warned "Not so fast!" and "Stop running!" By the time they enter kindergarten, they will have been cautioned and reminded to slow down for at least two years.

It is oddly reassuring to watch the nursery school children; it makes the most disconcerting kindergarten behavior seem quite natural and not the result of poor classroom management. I am drawn especially to a "tumbling room," furnished with gym mats and a small A-frame climbing ladder, adjacent to the nursery classroom. The inherent difference in momentum between boys and girls is never more clearly demonstrated than in that room.

On this particular day a group of three-year-old boys and girls have come in first. It is not a large area, and the maximum number of children allowed is six to eight—eight if it is mostly girls, six or less if boys are in the majority. Now three boys and four girls are there.

The boys run and climb the entire time they are in the room, resting momentarily when they "fall down dead." The girls, after several minutes of arranging one another's shoes, concentrate on somersaults. They continually say "Watch me" to the teacher, who smiles and nods. After a few somersaults, they stretch out on the mats and watch the boys. When the boys begin to run and jump on the mats, the girls move to the wall near the teacher. Occasionally a girl runs with the boys, but she stops after a few turns around the room. If she climbs the ladder, she sits on a middle rung or hangs from it. The boys scamper over her to the top, jump off, and continue to run. During a fifteen-minute period, there are six incidents of collisions and interference, none involving girls.

After one such tearful episode, the boys are sent back to the classroom, and the tumbling room suddenly belongs to the girls. The change is dramatic. With the boys gone, the girls run, climb, and tumble with a new vitality. No girl, though, runs more than twice around before coming to a halt, and each spurt of activity is followed by a longer, self-imposed rest.

"I have to get my dolly," says one girl, and thereafter when she rests on the mat, she dresses her doll. The idea spreads, two other girls running to retrieve their dolls. When doll play begins to supersede gymnastics, it is suggested the girls leave to make room for others. Throughout the period, boys are removed when they become too excited; girls leave when they appear to lose interest. No boy exits on his own, but about half of the girls decide they want to do something else. "Let's paint" or "Let's play in the doll corner" are the usual suggestions.

Next to enter is a group of three- and four-year-old boys. The older boys behave as do the younger ones, only more so. They run faster, climb higher, jump farther, and yell louder. Though the accelerated pace seems related to superhero play, the accompanying plots actually introduce a pacing effect not present before. The boys stop to argue the details of dramatis personae and use the climbing ladder as a space vehicle from which to shoot enemies. There is more symbolic action and less random running, all of which is copied by the younger boys. In the midst of a particularly noisy chase, the boys are told their time is up.

Two four-year-old girls look in and, seeing the room empty, run to notify four other girls. They push the mats together and begin to practice somersaults and cartwheels. One girl flips over several times without using her hands, and the others stop to watch. "My sister showed me," she tells them. "Put your hands in the back of you." All the girls try the new somersault with varying degrees of success, then drift over to the ladder, where they laugh and tease one another as they swing from its highest rungs.

"Do they ever just run around as the boys do?" I ask the teacher. "Oh, sure," she replies. "They'll run sometimes just to run, but then before you know it they're doing somersaults or trying headstands. Of course, if the boys are here, the girls don't stay long."

At this point, a few of the younger girls wander back in, still clutching their dolls. They watch for a while and then one says, "Show me how." The original no-hands tumbler takes great pains to demonstrate, helping the younger girls as long as they ask.

After a morning of sight-seeing in the tumbling room, I come away with a vivid picture of younger boys following older boys into superhero play and younger girls following older girls into gymnastics. I might be inclined to think the boys cannot somersault, whereas in fact most of them managed at least one and proved to be as proficient as the girls. They run because they prefer to run, and their tempo appears to increase in direct proportion to crowded conditions, noise levels, and time spent running, all of which have the opposite effect on the girls.

The habit of collisions is equally easy to trace: the boys do not watch where they are going. Either they don't notice the distance to the next person or they enjoy the impact too much to stop. All the boys tumbled on the mat without first making sure it was clear, while every girl but one looked in advance. In the older group, the gap between impulsive action and deliberate restraint was even more pronounced.

As I return to my classroom, the children run in from music. The girls are full of ominous reports:

"You should have saw how bad the boys were!"

"They got in trouble the whole time!"

I am surprised at my own pique. Here I have just spent an hour observing the raw energy of younger boys, and I still am annoyed and disappointed when my boys misbehave.

22 The boys have always gotten into trouble in music, but not more than during any other thirty-minute period in which they are prevented from playing and expected to alternate between sitting and moving. Girls are more successful at these times because they and the teacher usually travel at the same speed.

I might put on a cowboy record and ask everyone to gallop—for about three minutes. This is the approximate time nursery school girls ran in the tumbling room before coming to a natural halt. For boys, however, three minutes is only a beginning; the bigger the crowd, the faster they move and the longer they keep going.

To this difference in momentum add the fact that galloping may suggest a special choreography to boys, one that encourages bumping and grabbing.

"Where are the horses going?" I ask.

"To look for their mother," says Charlotte.

"I'm looking for bad guys," says Jonathan.

"Look for me! I'm a bad guy!" Andrew yells.

"Just a moment, boys. We're in the middle of rhythms. Save that for the playground," I say, stopping the boys' drama. I do not prevent the girls from developing *their* galloping drama, however. Mary Ann tells Charlotte she will be the mother, and they gallop hand in hand the next time around.

At the mention of bad guys the boys move into a chase, and I change the record to the "Blue Danube Waltz." The girls, whose horses slowed down even before the first record ended, glide along easily, but the boys find it hard to dismount. Caught in a clumsy position, they run, leap, and fall down. Their behavior has a domino effect, since they watch one another closely in awkward situations.

Would it have been better to begin with a waltz and change to a gallop? Transitions from slow to fast are always easier for boys; but, inevitably, whatever activity follows the gallop is met by a restless group—unless, that is, the activity is play. If the goal is physical harmony between boys and the environment, self-initiated play wins first place. Second honors go to the sort of play that is regulated by rules and painted lines. In free play the individual coordinates his own stops and starts. In gym games the rhythm is governed by explicit rules. Fantasy is carefully structured in one and is set aside in the other.

The Chinese New Year parade is an example of a mass fantasy with no place to go. When the boys play dragons in the block area, some of their energy is used to build caves and hideouts. Each boy sets his own pace. He may stop to join a checkers game or to paint a picture or listen to a record. He may decide to dictate a dragon story or look at a dragon book.

On the other hand, a playground game of dragons and giants follows well-known rules. Every step is decided by a giant who calls out the time of day. At "three o'clock" the dragons take three steps, at "eight o'clock" the dragons take eight, but at "twelve o'clock midnight" the giant gives chase. Extra steps are not allowed, and chaotic running meets with cries of "He's cheating!"

By contrast, the Chinese dragon was neither play nor sport. It stimulated monster fantasies without providing the outlets of ordinary play or the protection of concise rules. A fourteen-foot exploding dragon is hard to escape, and the school corridor, unlike the block area or the playground, symbolizes all the difficulties boys have in transition periods.

Shortly after the parade another event takes place that pushes the boys even further out of control. Jonathan brings his Star Wars record to school and near riot conditions occur during our Friday-afternoon rhythm period. We set aside this time each week because there is no music period on that day. Furniture is pushed against the walls to open up space for large-scale movement, and the children bring favorite records from home. After the Star Wars incident, by the way, we decide to use records from the school library only.

The boys have been staring at the album cover all morning with the same intensity they give their Darth Vader dolls. They seldom run with these little figures as they do when they have a car or stick in hand. Rather, they imagine that the figure itself is running or fighting. The boys sit and watch their tiny superhero dolls, giving the illusion of movement with soft, explosive sounds and whispered passwords: "It's the Death Star!" "He's got the Force!" "P-sh-sh!" No one moves; the excitement seems to remain inside the dolls.

The Star Wars record, however, worked in the opposite way. The moment it went on, the boys' inhibitions were released. When I describe the scene later to Jonathan's mother, she is surprised. "He's so quiet at home when he listens to it." Of course, he doesn't have twelve other boys at home.

Customarily a new record needs a brief introduction before

we move with the music. Star Wars needs none; as soon as it is played, everyone immediately imitates a flying machine. Arms out, heads pressed forward, the children fly around the room. Suddenly the boys turn on one another, leaping and screaming, "You're dead!" "I killed you first!" Robots run into spaceships, rockets destroy TIE fighters, storm troopers shoot at everyone. Each boy is fighting every other boy. Even Teddy is pulling someone down.

I take the record off quickly and order everyone to stop. "Sit down, please. Boys, you are entirely wild. We cannot have this. Now, watch the girls do it."

I put the record on again and the girls zoom and dip, looking like motorized butterflies. The boys nod their approval, but the moment they return to the floor they repeat their previous behavior, as if in a dream. Most of the girls leave the floor and find chairs along the wall, and I feel my anger mount.

"Rugs! Get your rugs! Now!" I shout, turning the record player and lights off at the same time. "We need a rest," I say in a softer voice. I reach for *Charlotte's Web* and turn to the chapter entitled "The Miracle." Lurvey, the hired man, has just discovered the words "Some Pig" printed in the web over the barn door, and Charlotte's plan to save Wilbur's life begins to unfold. The children stretch out or curl up on their rugs with visible relief. Zuckerman's barn is miles away from Star Wars.

The effect of the record was overwhelming. Such events cause teachers to outlaw superhero play forever. Next to arguments for or against workbooks, no subject is more controversial. Shall superhero play be allowed? Is it an outlet for tensions, or does it create new ones?

The answer to all three questions is a tremulous yes. For one thing, there is no way to prevent superhero dramas. The images will not go away; they stubbornly persist in a boy's head, bringing him pleasure and concern at the same time. The pleasurable aspects of the play help reduce tensions, which then build up again if make-believe aggression appears too real to the child or the teacher.

The balance between this seesaw rhythm and classroom

business is precarious, and the teacher is conditioned by the boys' behavior. I know, for example, that if we play outside before going to the library, the boys will not have settled down in time. On the other hand, if we have a math lesson before library time, too many fantasies are stored up lying in wait for the first excuse to erupt. Therefore I give in and let the children play indoors before library period or music or an assembly. There is an unspoken compromise: *The more you let us play, the better we will behave when we are not playing.*

I break my side of the compact more than they do. The fear that things will get out of hand prompts me to move in the opposite direction—away from free play. Tables and chairs, paper and pencils often seem more dependable as crowd controllers, but the benefits are fleeting. A boy who is displaced too often from play seeks relief in fantasy with increasing tenacity. When I misread the tension in the classroom and cut down on play, it works against the most effective tension reliever the children have.

23   We are about to act out Charlotte's story about two flowers who love each other, when Mary Ann suddenly places her head in Andrew's lap. Absentmindedly he strokes her hair and cradles her shoulder. Jonathan rolls his eyes and twirls about in his place on the circle, not knowing where to look. I too am caught by surprise, but no one else in the class acts as if anything unusual is happening.

Mary Ann says "Stay here, Andrew" and joins Charlotte in her story-play:

> Once upon a time there was two flowers and they
> loved each other. They loved to stay all by
> themselves. They had a lot of fun together.

At the end of the story, Mary Ann resumes her reclining

position and Andrew again smoothes her hair. Had he been asked to caress her in a play, he would have laughed and made faces. However, no one laughs at the two children. The differences between story-play characters and real people are understood by everyone.

When we finish the morning's stories, Andrew remains seated until Mary Ann gets up. Then he runs to the block area, where Jonathan is building the final section of a spaceship.

"Pretend we're Shogun warriors," Andrew says. "You have to walk like this. Pretend we're giants. Pretend I'm in trouble. When I go 'Wha-wha-wha,' you have to come. Okay?"

"Pretend we're armies," Jonathan counters. "Pretend we're being bombed. Pretend you're watching me to see if I'm dead."

"Pretend we're Shogun warriors," Andrew repeats, adding blocks to a tower. "Pretend I'm a robot and I just made you. You were just born and you can never break and you have to do whatever I say. Lie down!"

"I'm an army man," Jonathan informs him.

"Okay. You can be an army man or a robot. If you're a robot you have to do what I say."

"Okay. I'm a robot," Jonathan says.

In the doll corner, Mary Ann and Charlotte are setting the table.

"Baby, come eat."

"I'm in a hurry."

"Don't rush. Go dry your hands, baby."

"Mommy, Mommy, my cup. Where's my soup?"

"Yum, yum, I'm eating my nuts."

"I'm putting these things away."

"Ding-dong. Come in."

"It's a witch. Ask for a drink."

"Pretend it's poison. Tell her not to drink it."

"Mama, don't drink it."

"Let's wash these cups."

"Look, I see a kitty cat. It's sleeping."

"Pretend we're going to the ball. Pretend you just got a letter."

"Pretend you're married to someone."

"Pretend you're in my power. I'm the queen."

"I have magic, too."

"You have to do what I say. Go and fetch some wood! Do you want to be the baby? Okay. Come here, little baby. I'll comb you. I'll rock you. Oh, poor baby is so sad. Oh, oh."

It is easy to find comfort in the doll corner. By comparison, the block area appears cold and impersonal. Shogun warriors and robots speak in gruff, mechanical tones; they do not pet each other or talk of sadness. Yet these dramas, I am suddenly aware, include many tender scenes. Jonathan watches Andrew die and then revives him. Andrew gives himself a maternal role, with Jonathan as the newborn robot who can never be broken. And, of course, they continually rescue each other:

> Luke said "Help!" and Han brought him his light
> saber. Then he tried to find the storm troopers. But
> he fell in the Trash Compactor. "Help!" Luke
> brought a giant magnet and then he pulled him out.
> Then they both looked for Darth Vader. (Andrew)

The boys go off looking for Darth Vader with the same sense of well-being as two little girls on a picnic. They can yell "Help!" as often as Baby cries "Mommy!", and the dying superhero is given the same gentle concern as the little sister whose kitten is lost in the woods.

Friendship is by now the dominant theme, and Charlotte's dancing princesses and flowers who love each other have no monopoly. After two days of playing Shogun warriors, Andrew and Jonathan put the experience into story form, albeit in somewhat different versions:

> Once there were two Shogun warriors and one was
> a giant. When he went "Wha-wha-wha," the other
> one had to come. Then he made a robot. When he
> went "Wha-wha-wha," the robot brought him a
> poison-dart gun. Only the giant could have a robot.
> (Andrew)

> There was two army men and they didn't have

bullets. Then they found bullets. Then they killed the Shogun warrior, but he came alive again. Then they both decided to be army men and not Shogun warriors. And they didn't ever have robots in that army. (Jonathan)

Shogun warriors and army men are surely brothers who love each other. Once I recognize this fact, the shooting takes on a friendlier sound.

24

This morning the girls' play is full of robbers and police. The scene shifts raucously back and forth between the doll corner and the horizontal ladder. They shriek "Let's hide! They're after us!" and clomp in high heels to the ladder, from which they hang by their knees until someone mentions "baby." Then everyone runs back to the doll corner. This is the way it sounds:

Upside-down on the ladder:

"Pretend there's a stranger."

"Pretend we're running away."

"Pretend I'm a robber. If you kill someone, you have to marry the other person. Pretend you're in my power."

"Pretend I have a gun."

"Pretend you're a regular baby. Come on, baby, take your nap."

The girls run into the doll corner:

"Here's the bottle. Go to sleep."

"Lock the door."

"I want to be the stranger."

"Pretend the kitty cat wakes you up."

"Emergency 411. I hear robbers."

"Let's hide. They're after us!"

The doll corner empties and the girls are back on the ladder:

"I'm the leader of the police station. Kill the robbers because they killed the beautiful princess."

"Pretend I'm the queen of the police station."

"I'm the police sister."

"Call the sheriff. Tell him we hear a monster."

"Pretend the boys are scaring us."

"Pretend we have babies."

Everyone returns to the doll corner:

"We each have two babies."

"Pretend we're the babies."

"No, let's only just be sisters. No babies and no mothers."

"Operator, operator. Call the police. There's a sound on the phone. We have to get out. Get your purse. Don't call anyone. We have to hide."

The group reassembles under the ladder:

"I'm a valentine superhero."

"I'm a valentine supervalentine!"

"Pretend we're sisters and the superheroes are looking for us."

"Pretend this is really a castle."

"I'm the queen of the police station."

"Go back to your house. The baby is crying."

Andrew: Can we play?

Charlotte: Yes, but don't make noise. The baby is sleeping.

Jonathan: We're aliens. Take one more step. I'll shoot you.

Mary Ann: No. You have to say "Pretend we have babies."

Paul: We're the babies.

Mary Ann: No. Say "*Pretend* we have babies."

Paul: I'm a wild bronco.

Andrew: You be Big Hulk. I'm Little Hulk.

Jonathan: I'm the pet dinosaur. Pretend I'm scaring the girls.

Mary Ann: Get out! Only the girls are scaring people. You can't play. Out! Out!

The boys leave uncertainly but without protest. Their quick exit surprises and excites the girls, who run around the circle, flushed and happy, shouting, "Supervalentines!"

"Girls! Stop that! You're much too loud!"

"Okay. We won't be."

"No. Either play on the ladder or in the doll corner. This running back and forth is entirely too noisy."

"But the robbers are coming!"

"Do that part outside."

"We can't! It's too big outside."

There are too many people outside, the girls are telling me, and too large a space. In this room there is a governable balance between safety and danger. They can run from strangers and robbers—or become strangers—without fear of being chased. They can inhabit the jailhouse and still touch base in the doll corner. Everything is better controlled inside the classroom, where all the familiar distractions and symbols of domestic life are nearby.

My response to the girls' spirited play is less than cordial. Any resolve to promote more active play among the girls disappears with their first stampede across the room. What I had in mind for them was energetic block building and more aggressive kick ball, not cops and robbers.

The girls wait for my answer: Will they be allowed to run and shout in the classroom? It is an issue I face with ambivalence. Sometimes I treat running as a natural phenomenon and at other times as the enemy. Mood, not logic, seems to be the determining factor. The children are aware of my inconsistencies and try to persuade me.

"If we whisper, then can we do it?"

"Okay. Close the door," I tell them. "Then you can do it."

They are surprised. The door is always open. I come from a teaching model that views an open door as proof that the teacher has nothing to hide.

"I don't want to disturb the children who are studying," I say. They have cause to doubt my sincerity, since the closest classroom to the kindergarten is seventy five feet away. The fact is I do not want the world to witness a chaotic-looking scene. I know it is not really chaotic, that a well-developed story is in progress, but I recoil at any possible implication that I have lost control.

What I worry about is not control but the *appearance* of control. Instead of asking myself, "Is running a natural and necessary part of a five-year-old's indoor play?" I ask, "What will people think?"

A gym class is noisier than any kindergarten room, yet the gym teacher appears always in command. We expect children to run and shout in the gymnasium, but we are not so certain what good preschool play looks like. The presence of doll corners and block areas encourages fantasy play, but a natural and predictable consequence of that play is the contravention of the oldest school commandment: Thou shalt not run in school.

If a "robber" chases you, must you even then walk? According to school logic, you may run if he is chasing you in a printed script, but neither of you may run in free play. You may run outside, where lack of restraint and crowded conditions promise frequent collisions, but not inside, where everyone is more careful. I continue to insist that robbers belong on the playground, when all the children know that robbers come indoors to steal things.

The child reasons: There are characters who must run and those who should skip; some crawl and others cook supper or put people in jail or go up in rockets. Everything depends on what you are playing and with whom, not on the location.

Some of the best written-down stories are occasioned by the noisiest indoor play. Janie, for example, conceives her finest story after the tumultuous "supervalentine" scene on the climbing ladder:

> Once there lived a family of valentines. There was
> a mother and a sister and a baby. It was almost
> valentine season. They were scared. They heard
> dangerous noises. They locked the doors and
> windows. Robbers wanted to steal real valentines
> that were alive. The hunter found them and tried to
> get in, but he couldn't open the door. Then another
> hunter came, but he couldn't open the door, either.
> Then the hunter set a trap so when they came out
> they would be stuck. So they went out and almost got

caught, but they ran to the police station because
their mother was queen of the police. It was real
valentine police. Then they ran back inside before
the hunter could get them, because it was time for
dinner. So they ate supper and the doors were
locked. But the telephone rang, but they didn't
answer. Then the hunters never came back. The
father valentine came home from work and he didn't
know what happened.

As I read Janie's story aloud, the actors run around inside
the circle, pretending to hide and locking windows and doors.
They scramble up the ladder to the police station, adding appropriate dialogue: "Help! I'm scared. Save me!" The au-
dience sits in silent concentration; I, too, am filled with admiration.

Could anything be more absurd? I ask myself. Am I content
when the children pretend to pretend, but not when they are
really pretending? Do I censure the doll-corner version and
applaud its facsimile on stage?

Of course, theater is more dependable than real life; conflict
is at a minimum and all parties appear to be in control. Janie
does not need to argue about who is the mother, the actors are
given predictable roles in a familiar context, and I, the teacher,
can, in good conscience, control physical exuberance. Script
in hand, I can limit silliness by continuing the narrative, and
stop the action by reading "The End."

While I ponder the convenience of theater, I am struck by
the obvious: Theater is merely pretend play. The vital force
that fuels the imagination comes from real play, not from the
neatly packaged copy in my hand.

Janie's valentine family is born out of her excitement as a
supervalentine. It was a deeply emotional experience for the
girls. They combined male and female symbols—super and
valentine—and celebrated their invention in a burst of joyful
running.

What was my purpose in stopping them? Who was bothered
by the loud voices and running? Those at the art table con-
tinued to paint, the players at the checkerboard concentrated

on their next moves, and Teddy, dictating his third Star Wars story in two days, looked up only when I rushed over to talk to the girls. Am I the only one who finds merit in a quiet room?

The moment I close the door, the room seems less noisy, even though the girls are now running around capturing bad valentines and putting them in jail. I notice a strange thing: The louder the girls, the quieter the boys. The noise level in the room remains the same.

I am somewhat uncomfortable with my decision to close the door, so I tape a sign on it: "Welcome to room 110. Don't bother to knock. Walk right in. We are playing and probably won't hear you."

25   With the door closed I am more permissive, yet the room is only a little noisier. The boys are noticeably more disruptive for a while—apparently waiting for me to quiet them—before they settle into their usual routines. Unquestionably I have been monitoring their behavior too much; they look my way when it becomes noisy. The girls are more confident that I won't interfere with their play. Several children continue to ask about the closed door:

> Teacher: I close it when the room is noisy.
> Charlotte: Because of the boys.
> Teacher: Sometimes the girls. Remember when you
>   were running back and forth to the ladder? That
>   was when I first closed the door, so you could
>   finish your police story.
> Andrew: Did you close it for Star Wars?
> Teacher: I'm sure I did.
> Paul: And for shooting?
> Teacher: I still don't like shooting in the classroom.
> Paul: How 'bout if it's quiet like this? P-a-h, p-a-h.
> Teacher: It's better if you do it outside.
> Jonathan: But we can't bring out things.

Teacher: That's the rule for everyone in the
   playground. Children run fast outside. If you're
   holding something and you fall, you could get hurt.
Andrew: We could hold something in the room
   because we don't run fast?

Andrew has touched on an inconsistency in my logic. Shooting is always safer indoors and just for the reasons he suggests. As there is less running, the boys have more self-
control.

Teddy: What if you walk? Then could you shoot?
Franklin: Use light sabers. They don't make noise.
   Wh-sh-sh.
Jeremy: No! Laser beams. That kills you really
   quietly.

The room is still; the last idea brings a reflective pause. The
subject, they think, is running and noise, not images of violence.

Teacher: It isn't just the noise, you know. Shooting is
   all about killing people. It looks wrong in a
   classroom.

Even as I speak, I realize my distinctions are shaky. Is there
a difference between "Pretend our parents are dead" and "Pre-
tend I'm killing you"? The children know it is all magical play.
The same magic destroys and resurrects, creates an orphan or
a mother—or the Green Slime. The ability to imagine some-
thing is the magic; putting it into action is the play; playing it
out is the safe way to discharge the idea.
   After the discussion, Andrew turns to Paul:
"Pretend this is bee land."
"No, pretend it's bat land."
"I'm the vampire."
"Pretend there's an explosion."
"Pretend the volcano is exploding."

"Pretend we're vampires and we got melted and we can't breathe."

Exciting images fill their heads during the discussion, and the boys can hardly wait for me to stop talking. They move around each other in a dreamy ballet, shooting at vague targets, murmuring little cries:

"I'm the vampire. You're Batman."

"You're a monster. I'm the Green Slime."

"I'm the Hulk. Pretend I killed you."

"No, you be the Green Slime. Pretend you killed my brother."

Now a chase begins that lasts about thirty seconds. Andrew zigzags between tables and chairs, waving a gun made of interlocking plastic squares. No one watches the boys except Jonathan, who calls out, "Can I play? I'm Luke!" Receiving no answer, he runs after them. "Who's the boss? I'm Luke!"

"We're not playing that. Anyway, you need a weapon."

"Okay. I'll be right back."

Andrew and Paul stop to watch a dice game, periodically taking aim at children crossing the room. "P-ing! Gotcha!" slips out as naturally as the constant appearance of gun-shaped objects in their hands.

Few of these boys have toy guns at home. In our community, social pressure weighs heavily against guns. Superhero paraphernalia is purchased but not guns. It is a prohibition, however, that has no effect on play. Even in nursery school, the boys pick up any loose item and shoot. When confronted with the "no-guns" rule, they insist they are holding a walkie-talkie. The euphemism is accepted and the children learn how to negotiate with the teacher. By kindergarten they are masters of guile.

"This isn't a gun," Andrew tells me even before I ask.

"It looks like a gun and sounds like a gun," I say.

"It's an invention."

"What does it do?"

"It X-rays people."

There is a new activity in the room: The children go out into the hall, knock on the door, and re-enter.

"What's going on?" I ask, annoyed. "The door keeps opening and closing."

"I heard a noise in the hall," Paul says.

"I think someone is calling me," Charlotte reports.

"Let's just leave the door open, then," I suggest. It is clear that the children do not like the closed door. Besides, I find that I want to know who is passing by in the hall.

Franklin remembers my reason for closing the door. "Do like you done before. Tell the bad guys to sit down to color."

Franklin's common-sense approach reminds me that there are no short cuts or gimmicks to logical classroom procedure. If Cinderella is acceptable but cops and robbers is not, I should be able to explain why—to myself and to the children.

What are these sensible rules I admire so much, and how does cops and robbers compare with Cinderella when it comes to following them?

The first rule says that a player or group of players may not disturb other players. This rule is hard for the boys, since the whole point of cops and robbers is to intrude and steal something, preferably in the doll corner. However, having watched the girls play strangers and police for three consecutive days, I can no longer accept at face value their complaints against the boys.

The girls could be more accommodating to the robbers were it not for the fact that the girls do not share space and materials—rule 2—as well as the boys. For instance, they do not wish to share any part of the doll corner when they are playing there. They refuse to allow the boys to steal dishes and food or to turn the doll corner into a hideout. Yet, when the girls build a house in the block area, they automatically take all the food, dishes, clothing, and bedding with them and insist that the boys share the blocks. Boys forfeit teacher support because they label their actions as "stealing." Were they to say instead that the girls were not "sharing," the teacher might come to their aid. But, of course, without "stealing," it is not cops and robbers.

A third rule concerns excessive noise and careless running, a problem for both Cinderella and the robber. High heels, crying babies, and runaway pets are as disruptive as the omnipresent bad guy; running is the same whether the runner is Cinderella or Luke Skywalker. Boys do, of course, run more—much more. However, they run more whether or not they are playing cops and robbers. Jonathan gets up and runs around the table every time he gets a king in checkers. I asked him once why he did it and he answered, "That's what you have to do when you get a king."

There is a final rule, applicable only to boys; no grabbing, pushing, punching, or wrestling. They are more likely to break this rule, however, when they line up, walk down the hall, get ready for lunch, or come to the circle—those in-between times when controls are least dependable.

Perhaps, then, instead of steering robbers and superheroes out of the classroom, I ought to help them improve their style. After all, stealing and shooting are stage business, not necessarily more in opposition to the rules of good play than the selfish behavior of the stepsisters who won't let Cinderella attend the ball.

26 Teddy is no longer a doll-corner resident; he is now a guest or an intruder there. As a guest, he responds to invitations—usually to be the father. All the boys, even Andrew, will agree to a brief stint as father if they are alone when asked.

The girls understand what turns a guest into an intruder: The magic number is 3. If one boy is summoned into the doll corner, he is likely to cooperate; two, in certain combinations, might still be manageable; three, never. Three boys form a superhero clique and disrupt play. The doll corner is easy to understand, for there is but a single drama to enter, as either protagonist, antagonist, or supporting player.

By contrast, the many unconnected activities in the block area must share the same space and materials, each unit continually readjusting its boundary lines to accommodate the others. A half hour of constructive play in the blocks requires one or more of three conditions: socially mature players, a plot strong enough to make role-playing more important than covetousness, or the presence of leaders with good building skills.

Believing that Franklin would do admirably well in all categories, I urge him to leave the art table and apply his talents to the block area. At both the art table and the wood-bench, he is the model of maturity and aplomb. He performs his self-appointed tasks with such meticulous care that others watch and copy him. His intense concentration on clearly defined goals entices more boys into "work" projects than all my curriculum ideas combined.

Much to our surprise—the children's and the teacher's—Franklin has the opposite effect in the blocks. There he is dictatorial and intolerant; his sense of perfection rules out any notion of group participation. Anything less than total control is an impossible compromise for him to make.

He has this control in art construction and, to some extent, in superhero play, where his detailed knowledge of movie and television scripts usually gives him the final word. In the block area, however, nothing matters so much as a democratic spirit, and Franklin does not yet have this. He ends every session in tears, and block play is in danger of being ruined.

I station myself outside the blocks to see if I can identify the point at which things go wrong. Ordinarily, by the time I arrive on the scene it is too late; everyone is angry and no one can explain what happened.

Jonathan is already building when Franklin runs in, asking, "Can I play?"

"Sure you can," Jonathan replies. "I'm building a house."

"Wait! Don't put it there!" Franklin grabs a block from Jonathan's hand and begins to rearrange the design of the building. "This is the way. Do it like this," he states firmly.

Jonathan tentatively lays a block on its side.

"No! Leave it alone! You're spoiling it!" Franklin yells again. "Just watch me, can't you?" He does not look at Jonathan as he speaks; he concentrates only on the blocks.

Teddy, who has been observing the scene, puts a large arc

at one corner of the building. He keeps his eyes on Franklin, testing to see what his friend will do.

"No, Teddy! That ain't the way it has to be!" Franklin removes the arc. "Lemme have that! Just put it away. We don't need it high over there! It don't look nice that way!"

I can no longer remain silent. "Franklin, you're very bossy. You won't let the boys do anything."

He looks surprised. "Yeah they can. I said they can."

"But you grab their blocks the minute they have an idea."

"I'm helping them. They want me to."

"Do you boys want him to?"

Jonathan and Teddy look at each other, but before they can speak, Franklin is crying and pulling Andrew's arm down: "Leave that be, Andrew! It's mine!"

Andrew looks as if he's going to hit Franklin with the block. With me there, all he can do is scream, "He wasn't even using it! He's a stupid pig!"

"I am so using that! It goes right here. I need all those. I was here first. You're spoiling my whole thing." Franklin tearfully runs back and forth to the block shelf, filling his arms with blocks as, one by one, the boys leave.

"Franklin, will you please look around," I say. "Everyone is gone."

"Why?"

"Why? Because you're being very selfish, that's why."

Franklin looks worried. "I ain't selfish. I ain't said they hasta go."

"You're just like the fox in 'The Blue Seed.' Remember that story? He wouldn't let anyone share his house, so the house blew up?"

Franklin nods, squinting to take the measure of his building. "Can I finish my house now?"

The moral of the fox story is of no concern to Franklin. The offending party never sees the connection to his own behavior in a morality tale.

"Franklin, wait. Let me tell you what I mean about the fox," I say, determined to press my point. "Remember when you were the fox? You had to yell at everyone, 'Get out! You can't live in my house!' That's just what you're doing in the blocks now."

"I ain't doin' that! Soonest I'm done, everyone can come in. First I gotta get it just right."

"But they want to help."

"I said they can help. They wasn't listening."

My approach is useless. He can picture every detail of the ten-story house he plans to erect but nothing of the scene he just had with Jonathan and Teddy. Yet Franklin knows how to listen to dialog and stay in character. When he is the father in the doll corner, he does not act like Darth Vader. Nor does he make the little pig sound like the Big Bad Wolf. Artistic integrity is important to Franklin. What he needs is an objective view of the scene he just played. The analogy of the selfish fox is too abstract and direct criticism too personal. The storyplays come to mind: "Once there was a boy named Franklin. . . ."

The class is seated around the circle. I have asked Jonathan and Teddy to bring a pile of blocks into the center.

"This is a guessing game," I tell everyone. "I'm acting out a true story. You have to guess who I'm pretending to be. You two boys pretend you're building something, and I'm going to keep interrupting."

Self-consciously the boys begin to build a road. I rush over and grab several blocks. "No, not that way! Give it here! Do it this way!" I shout.

The boys are momentarily startled but continue to lay out blocks. I yell at them again: "Stop doing it that way! You're spoiling my road!"

By now everyone is looking at Franklin, who is pounding his thigh and laughing. "That's me! You're pretending you're me! Is that really me?"

"It really is you. I watched you in the blocks. That's the way you sounded. Remember?"

"I do remember! You did that part just right."

When I confronted Franklin earlier in the block area, he denied everything. The moment I make him the star in his own story, he is flattered and attentive. He is not offended and therefore does not need to defend himself. My view of objectivity is the opposite of the children's. They can become objective only when events are seen as make-believe.

"Okay, Franklin, now you come into the circle. I pretended to be you. Now you pretend to be a boy named Franklin who lets people use their own ideas in the blocks. 'Once upon a time there was a boy named Franklin who knew how to play in the blocks.'"

Franklin saunters out, grinning broadly, and starts to build a tower. I motion to Jonathan and Teddy to help him.

"That's good, boys," he says, nodding agreeably. "You sure got good ideas. Go on, get some more good ideas."

Everyone claps. It is a grand performance, reminiscent of the finale to "The Blue Seed." The fox is gone; long live Virtue!

Lasting changes in behavior are not so easily achieved, of course. But, in kindergarten, appearances are important. Suddenly I recognize the difference between telling a child he must share and saying instead, "Pretend you are a boy who knows how to share." The first method announces that a child has done something wrong. "Pretend" disarms and enchants; it suggests heroic possibilities for making changes, just as in the fairy tales.

27   A role-playing incident may not alter a person's manners, but it provides a standard for easy reference. I can now speak about Franklin's behavior in a calm context, and he willingly sees himself in the picture. Cops and robbers could also benefit from an approach that omits dispiriting confrontations. My normal response, when robbers charge the doll corner, is to ignore the plot and remove the characters from the stage, thereby changing the subject from fantasy to recrimination.

"You boys cannot spoil the girls' play," I say. They reply, "We're robbers," but I dismiss the notion. "You can't be robbers," I tell them, implying that pretending to be robbers is as bad as really being robbers. Yet, a professional actor is not taken to be the villain he portrays; he is judged by his acting. Perhaps I can do more to promote this idea with the girls.

> Teacher: I've been thinking about cops and robbers. Remember when the girls complained that the boys were not being fair in the blocks and then the boys began to share more often? Well, the girls are not being fair to the boys in the doll corner.
> Andrew: I don't want to play in the doll corner.
> Teacher: Sometimes you want to play cops and robbers there.
> Andrew: Oh, you mean that.
> Charlotte: They can't, right?
> Teacher: So far that's our rule. Then the boys forget and there's a big fuss. But, after all, aren't they acting out a story the same way the girls do?
> Mary Ann: They have to do theirs outside.
> Teacher: But no one tells *you* where to play Cinderella. When you build a Cinderella house in the blocks, the boys don't object.
> Mary Ann: If we're in the blocks, they can go in the doll corner.
> Teacher: They could, but when you're in the doll corner, you won't share the space.
> Charlotte: You can't give a piece of a house.
> Teddy: Only if it's a gingerbread house.
> Teacher: What if the boys said, "The blocks are only for Star Wars"?
> Charlotte: They can't do that.
> Jonathan: We can pretend we're eating the gingerbread house.
> Charlotte, Okay. We'll play "Hansel and Gretel." They can be the father or Hansel.
> Teacher: But what if they want to be robbers? Is there a way it can be done?
> Clarice: In the cubby room.
> Andrew: We can't take things out of people's cubbies.

Charlotte: Well, you can't steal from the doll corner.
That's only for playing house.
Jill: They spoil everything. They're too wild.
Mary Ann: And they don't leave when that part is
over.
Teacher: You mean it would be all right if they rob
only for a few minutes?
Charlotte: No way! We know what they do. They
keep doing it.
Teacher: The boys want to pretend to be cops and
robbers. They're not really rough—they never push
you, do they?—and they don't really steal. It's all
pretend, just like Cinderella. But we pretend they
are *real* robbers and chase them out and yell at
them.

No one has a response, but it is clear the boys like being
talked about. They look as if I have just complimented them
for some unusual display of restraint. The girls, however, are
fidgety as always when I ask them to change doll-corner
customs. It is a difficult task, because the first rule of the doll
corner is that everything must be pretend. No one enters or
leaves without preserving the continuity of make-believe.

Charlotte, for example, is in the crib when she realizes she
has to go to the bathroom. "Pretend I have to go," she says.

"Go in your potty."

"Pretend I *really* have to go."

"Oh. See you later, honey. Be sure to call."

When Charlotte returns she says, "I went to the ball. The
prince was there."

It doesn't matter that she switches to Cinderella. The thread
of magic remains intact.

Is superhero play inherently outside this protective fencing,
or do the girls simply reflect adult attitudes about boys' play?
Perhaps I miss the point: The intrusion by males and the ex-
pulsion by females may be a necessary ritual. If so, then it is
not the script that needs changing but my view of what is
happening.

The following week I pay close attention to the doll corner, observing the sort of conflict girls are willing to accept when they play there. I am impressed by the amount of antisocial behavior that occurs without disrupting the ongoing story: All sorts of pesty characters have tantrums; sisters quarrel, babies cry and throw dishes on the floor, pets topple chairs, mothers threaten and spank. No one finds these stock situations upsetting; they worry only about unfair sharing practices. "She won't let me be the mother! She's always the mother!"

I discover another interesting fact: The girls are at least as messy as the boys. Disorder and noise go unheeded; the girls may even prefer the haphazard piles strewn over the floor. Nothing ever gets cleaned up unless someone pretends to be a maid or the teacher insists.

Surely, then, it is not the commotion of cops and robbers that is offensive to the girls, but rather the fact that the game goes beyond the messy, jealousy-ridden, disagreeable, exciting havoc of ordinary doll-corner play. It introduces an element that is apparently not acceptable to girls—the evil outsider.

Robbers and strangers, ghosts and monsters are talked about, overheard, run away from, and locked out; but they do not appear in person. Even when girls can exert complete control—as in storytelling—they permit only brief glimpses of intruders. The girls may pretend that bad guys are about to enter the house, but the rule is strict: They must be kept out. Forceful entry results in unhappiness for the girls.

My investigation seems to have changed nothing; the boys still cannot rob the doll corner. Yet the perspective is different. Robbers must stay out, not because the boys behave badly, but because the two stories do not mesh. The integrity of fantasy must be preserved. In this the boys and girls are in complete agreement.

> Teacher: I've been watching the doll corner and I'm
> certain that the girls are telling the truth about
> cops and robbers. It really does make them feel
> bad. Think of it this way. What if a girl went into

that spaceship over there and told the boys, "I'm
the mother. You're the babies. Everyone go to
bed!"? You'd probably say, "No! You're spoiling
our story. We don't play that way."
(Everyone laughs.)
However, just because cops and robbers can't be
played in the doll corner doesn't mean it can't be
played. After all, it's an interesting story that lots of
people enjoy, even grownups. So, how about in the
blocks?

Charlotte: They can build a house and rob it.

Paul: Who is in the house to rob?

Mary Ann: Let Teddy be in the house. You wouldn't
care, okay, Teddy?

Teddy: Maybe I would.

Franklin: Teddy and me, we'll make a house, okay?
They can rob it. But then we rob them back
because we're really robbers, too.

Teacher: See how it works out. And let the girls give
you a few things from the doll corner.

The girls look at one another questioningly, wondering if
they dare yield an inch of territory.

Charlotte: Okay. But we have to give it to them. They
can't rob from us.

28   Once the cops-and-robbers issue has the appearance of being settled, the girls begin a
new kind of play that recaptures the excite-
ment of the supervalentine period. It makes subtle fun of superhero bravado and gives danger a gentle disguise. The
ideas are borrowed from a television program called "Scooby
Doo."
"Who's Scooby Doo?" I ask.

Charlotte is amazed by my ignorance. "He's a dog! On television!"

I am interested at once, for until now the girls have ignored all television characters. It is the boys who transpose the cartoons and police stories into usable material. Television gives them what fairy tales and domestic events offer girls: a continual flow of characters and actions. If the girls do not act out television programs, it is because ordinarily the subject matter does not suit doll-corner play.

In Scooby Doo, Charlotte finds an answer to a supervalentine question: Is there a nonthreatening way to include danger in the doll corner? According to Scooby Doo, the solution is simple, since danger is only a mystery that needs to be solved. There is a glow of recognition when the girls hear Charlotte's first Scooby Doo story:

> One day Princess Leia and Cinderella had a tea party. After that they went for a walk and met Scooby Doo. They said, "Hi, Scooby. Are you looking for a clue?" He said, "Yes, I'm after a mystery. A ghost is somewhere. That's why I'm walking this way." "Do you want to come to a party?" said Cinderella. "Who's having a party?" "It's all yours, Scooby. It's your birthday." So they all went to the party.

Scooby Doo, I learn, belongs to four teenagers who solve mysteries. Their names are Velma, Daphne, Fred, and Shaggy. Charlotte explains the general outline in her second story:

> Once upon a time there was a family that they always had to go out and solve mysteries. All of their names are Shaggy, Scooby Doo, Fred, Velma, and Daphne. They had to solve a mystery today. It has to be a ghost mystery. Daphne fell into a trap with Fred. Velma, Shaggy, and Scooby got lost. Then Scooby and Shaggy saw a ghost. "The ghost got me!" Then they ran away. But Velma found them. It wasn't a ghost. It was Mr. Johnson.

Judging from the stories that follow, a cast description would include Scooby Doo, a dog, and Shaggy, a boy, both easily frightened; Velma, strict and unflappable in the manner of queens or teachers; Daphne, the younger sister or princess type; and Fred, a well-behaved male much like the prince in Cinderella.

There is always an unknown danger, followed by an easily escapable trap, a fearful retreat, and a calm resolution. The male characters usually run away, and the females solve the mysteries.

Halfway through every story, Scooby and Shaggy frantically shout, "The ghost got me!" At this point, Velma exposes, disarms, or belittles the menace.

> Once there was Velma and Fred and Daphne and
> Scooby Doo. Scooby found a mystery. Then they fell
> in an underground cave. Then Scooby pushed on a
> wall. Then Scooby looked in a mirror and saw a ghost
> face, but he ran away. "The ghost got me!" Velma
> told him it's a fake ghost, but he ran away again.
> "The ghost got me!" So Velma called a good witch.
> She took him on her broom and away they went.
> (Mary Ann)

What is remarkable to me is that most of the girls choose to be Scooby rather than Velma. By taking the role of a mildly naughty, excessively cowardly boy dog, the girls seem to be mocking themselves and the boys as well.

The boys are not interested in this particular satire. They want male heroes who are fearless and superhuman.

> Teacher: All of a sudden the girls are telling so many
>   Scooby stories.
> Jonathan: I know why. Because Charlotte likes
>   Scooby Doo and the girls like Charlotte.
> Teacher: Maybe a boy will tell one.
> Andrew: They're girl stories.
> Teacher: Scooby is a boy. So are Shaggy and Fred.
> Andrew: But not superheroes.

Teacher: They have scary ghost adventures.

Teddy: Scooby and Shaggy get scared. Velma doesn't.

Teacher: She's sort of like a superhero.

Franklin (laughing): Naw! She's just a girl. Just a plain girl, that's all.

Scooby Doo is indeed a girl's story. The boys dismiss the characters as too lightweight, not because the girls have used the story first, as I once might have thought, but because the characters do not fit into the boys' fantasies. If the boys behaved in the Scooby manner, they would be included more often in doll-corner play, but the price would be too high. They cannot afford to become doll-corner pets.

> Once upon a time a little girl had a dog named Scooby Doo. The dog said, "The ghost got me" and he ran away. But the girl said, "No ghosts are here. That's my bunny rabbit." So he came back and she gave him Scooby snacks. (Clarice)

It is unfair to imply that boys do not like satire. In their stir-crazy stories, for example, they eagerly make fun of common notions of good behavior. Superhero deportment, however, is not questioned. The boys have too recently emerged from the doll corner to stand aside and view the superhero with humor.

29

Jill tells a Scooby Doo story that is different from the others. Its sober message instantly captures the serious attention of all the children:

> Once there was a little dog named Scooby and he got lost in the woods. He didn't know what to do. Velma couldn't find him. No one found him.

The most vulnerable hero imaginable is one who is lost in the woods. If a nursery school child tells the story, he is found speedily by loving parents who take him home and put him to bed. Sometimes he must first be taken to the hospital because he has been run over by a train, a condition that causes the parents to behave even more affectionately: "They carried him home from the hospital until he was well."

In kindergarten, there is an important change in the status of the lost child: The parents are dead. Now the lost child finds new parents who are nicer. If only one parent is dead, the child discovers the path to the other parent and brings blueberries picked in the woods or a lion shot for dinner, depending on the sex of the storyteller. Unhappy endings, such as Jill's, are rare, but if a child feels sad, sometimes the hero remains lost.

By midyear most lost children are girls, for the boys are preoccupied with their superheroes. Lost girls no longer search for parents; they decide to live in the woods in an empty house surrounded by flowers, or they meet a prince and live in a palace. The lost child is seen not as a victim but as a person about to make a change for the better.

Superheroes, of course, do not get lost in the woods, although sometimes they are lost in space. Luke Skywalker and Han Solo frequently search for each other and, once found, go off to look for someone else. In dozens of stories, superheroes do little else than try to locate each other, but the friends never settle down to live in one place. The absence of a permanent home is one of the biggest differences in boys' and girls' play. Even so, the idea of a little house in the woods has appeal for boys as well as for girls. The proof comes unexpectedly in a library book that turns the boys into doll-corner characters and allows them to enjoy some of the homey pleasures denied to superheroes.

The Boxcar Children, by Gertrude Chandler Warner, is the story of four homeless children who run away to avoid being sent to live with an unknown grandfather. The orphans turn an abandoned boxcar in the woods into a dream house, furnishing it with makeshift objects much as the girls stock their temporary dwellings built of blocks.

Even more compelling than the boxcar are the siblings themselves: The unstinting love and care given to Benny, at five years of age, fulfills every child's deepest wish. Here are brothers and sisters who transfer all the attention they might otherwise bestow on parents or friends to their little brother. Together they live in the woods without hint of jealousy or regret, performing all the functions of family life played out every day in the doll corner.

Henry, the oldest, goes to work in a nearby town to provide food for the family, Jessie and Violet cook and wash the dishes, and Benny picks blueberries in the woods. Everyone helps to make a wagon for Benny, since little children must have toys, even in the woods.

We finish the book in a week, but the children insist I read it again. They want to see if such a perfect story will be the same on second reading. The runaways, of course, are eventually found by a doting, rich grandfather, but the happy ending is superfluous. The class is interested only in the house in the woods, and continually repeats the act of making a boxcar into a home.

Everyone wants a turn to be Benny, and apparently the roles are distributed fairly, since I am seldom called to monitor the action. Henry, Jessie, Violet, and Benny set high standards for their readers; the youthful heroes solve their problems without adult help. During boxcar play, arguing is at a minimum and so is superhero activity. The class is too busy collecting discarded soda cans, empty milk cartons, rusty nails, and dandelions from the school playground to equip the boxcar.

The essential element is self-reliance. The children create a home and supply their own necessities. Months earlier I attempted, unsuccessfully, to legislate similar ideas in the doll corner when I removed store-bought items and asked the girls to provide for themselves. My plan failed, I see now, because it lacked a reason, a story. It was part of no one's fantasy in an area in which fantasy is the primary motivation.

After a few days, Andrew brings his Star Wars figures to

school and the boys step back into superhero roles. The girls continue to be boxcar children, blending the plot into ordinary doll-corner play. At no time during the original boxcar play did the girls seem surprised by the boys' exemplary behavior, but once back in the doll corner, they immediately assume the separateness that normally prevails. The children know one another better than do the teachers. Boys and girls pretend to accept appearances as reality, but in fact it is the adult who is fooled. The girls recognize that the tough superhero is the same little brother who lives at home and is often very much like Benny.

30

The Boxcar Children was a halcyon digression. Had I a magic wand, I might turn the boys in the class permanently into Bennys and Henrys.

Teacher: I miss Benny and Henry. And Jessie and Violet, too. I liked watching you act out that story.
Charlotte: You want us to do it again?
Teacher: Only if you want to.
Andrew: You could read about it in the book.
Teacher: Right. That's what I'll do. Do you boys ever think about Benny and Henry?
Jonathan: Yeah. Like when Violet told Benny to pretend he's a teddy bear.
Teacher: At the beginning when they're running away?
Andrew: Oh, yeah, that's good. He's too tired and then he pretends he's a bear.
Franklin: And then he pretends he's a horse. Right?
Teacher: Did you ever act out that part?
Andrew: Plenty of times we did. (Everyone smiles and nods at Andrew.)

The children refer to two minor incidents before the boxcar

is found, the only times when Benny is fussy. In the first, he is tired and wants to be carried, but Violet says, "Now, Benny, you can play you are a little brown bear running away to find a nice, warm bed." Later, when the thirsty children drink from a pump, Benny insists he needs a cup, and Henry tells him, "You can play you are a horse." The boys like Benny best when he has to pretend in order to be good.

They know Benny is being manipulated, yet they do not object. On the contrary, they are glad Benny's family understands the role of fantasy in accomplishing difficult tasks. The boys themselves need the boxcar fantasy to achieve a brief respite from the superhero.

And what of the girls? The boxcar adventure would seem to be their very own, indistinguishable from doll-corner play. Yet the peaceful contentment of the home in the woods is as illusory for girls as for boys. There is often more quarreling in the doll corner than in a spaceship. The quality of virtue at the kitchen table is dramatized in painfully realistic terms: good and bad children versus good and bad mothers. A solitary boy playing in the doll corner resembles Benny or Henry more than the girls do Violet or Jessie.

In trying to sort out what is real from pretend, one looks through mirrors that see into other mirrors. I choose books that seem relevant, but it is the children who operate the mirrors and make connections. Reflections of a recurrent dream are brought to life for the boys in the pages of *The Boxcar Children,* enabling them to band together with the girls, in girls' territory, without embarrassment or camouflage.

The girls experience a similar reincarnation several weeks later when I read Frank Baum's *The Wizard of Oz,* a story that is best known through the movie version. One can always tell when the film is presented on television, because suddenly Dorothy and the good witch Glenda appear in the doll corner. Now, however, as the children listen to the original story, another character takes hold of the girls. It is one that is a stranger to their play: the Wicked Witch of the West—Darth Vader with a broom.

Strong, masterful characters are not unknown to the girls, Mother being the best example. Princess Leia and Wonderwoman often join the boys, but a delicate balance is maintained. They fly in and out of boys' play with the elusiveness of butterflies, fluttering back to the other girls the moment the boys pursue them too seriously. Furthermore, these superwomen, entirely virtuous, are little different from the good mother or sister in the doll corner.

The Wicked Witch of the West rules a band of winged monkeys who perform her evil deeds. A scene erupts on the playground during which each girl is a powerful master and every boy a subservient robotlike monkey.

"Here—I—am—what—do—you—want."

"Go over there and kill everyone in the sandbox!"

"O—kay—now—what—is—your—e—vil—com—mand?"

"Knock down the jungle gym!"

The witches scream in unison as the hapless monkeys run back and forth carrying out their orders. The other children on the playground stop to watch the novel performance. Molly, a first grader, sits next to me on the bench.

"What is Charlotte playing?"

"The Wizard of Oz."

"Is she the Wizard?"

"I think the girls are wicked witches."

"Oh. I get it. The boys are monkeys?"

"It seems that way. Do you want to play?"

"I just want to watch."

"Do you like the way they're playing?"

"Yeah, I like it. I'm going to play that with my brother when I get home."

Unless you are playing with your little brother at home, bad characters need reinforcements. None of the girls would be a wicked witch by herself. The boys have been teaching this lesson to girls for years: There cannot be too many superheroes once you leave the doll corner.

31 Mary Ann still has witches on her mind the next day and exorcises one in a complicated story:

Once upon a time there lived two princesses who were prettier than ever and roser than a rose. They went to the woods. They saw the wicked witch hiding and she tried to catch them, but they were too fast. Then they went to the woods again. The wicked witch tried to catch them again. Luckily she did. She put them in a cage. There were no windows and doors. They could not breathe, so they died. . . . But that was a cage where it was raining gold. It woke them up. The gold was magic and it made a door and then they went home. Then two princes knocked on the door. When the princesses saw them they wanted to marry them, so they got married.

"Why do you say 'luckily'?" I ask. "Is it lucky that the witch catches the princesses?"

"No, lucky the cage is raining gold."

"Then do you want to say, 'Luckily that was a cage where it was raining gold'?"

"No. Then it will be too late. It has to be 'luckily' when she catches them."

No matter how risky their play may become, the girls take few chances in stories. They buffer the effect with roses and pretty princesses, cause cages to rain gold and princes to knock at the door. Charlotte tells a story in which she uses the word "pretty" eight times:

Once upon a time there was a princess prettier than a flower. She walked under a pretty rainbow. Then she met a prince and they went to a ball and the prince got the prettiest princess a flower. So she got another pretty dress and put the flower on it. Then all the princes at the ball wanted to dance with her, but she went to the prettiest prince. So he gave her another flower. So the prettiest princess married the prettiest prince and in the night she had the prettiest baby, so she told the prince what happened.

"I'm going to do one of these 'pretty' stories," Janie decides:

> Once there was a pretty girl and she planted pretty
> flowers in her pretty garden. And she was very
> pretty. Her name was Snow White. Then a witch
> gave her a poison apple, so she died. Then a pretty
> diamond necklace came on her neck and she came
> alive and she was still pretty.

"Pretty" is a magic charm, and, for a while, witches will be
foils to prove the power of prettiness.

> Once upon a time there were two pretty bunnies.
> Their mother said they could go for a walk. Then
> they saw a wicked witch and she killed them by her
> look. Then two prince rabbits came. Then two pretty
> lovebirds sang outside and woke up the pretty
> bunnies. So they married ever after. (Karen)

"Teddy, do you remember your story about a boy named
Pretty?" I ask.
"I remember." He is silent for a moment. "I still know a boy
named Pretty."
"Who is it?"
"Me. My grandma calls me her pretty boy."
"She must love you a lot."
"She does."

32 When "pretty" stories are at their zenith,
Charlotte switches back to Scooby Doo and
invents Superbrother, whose function is to
watch for robbers:

> Scooby Doo and Velma met Superbrother in the
> woods. Scooby said, "Did you see any robbers?"
> Superbrother said, "If I see any I'll tell you. Okay. I

see some. They're running that way." So they went
the other way until they came to Snow White's
house.

Charlotte is not afraid to try out ideas with a male stamp. It
is unlikely that a boy would create Supersister. Except for
commercial celebrities such as Princess Leia and Wonderwoman, boys scrupulously disregard female characters. Noncon-
formity rarely causes problems for a girl, since she is allowed
so wide a range of acceptable behavior. She can play in any
fashion without embarrassment. A boy in a frilly bedjacket expects to be laughed at, but a superhero cape on a girl creates
no stir. There is nothing illusory about female adaptability—or
male intransigence—in matters of fantasy play.

If boys are inflexible in "pretend play," they are even more
so in "pretend school." Most table activities devised by the
teachers during free play are welcomed by the girls and rejected by the boys. "They don't know what they are saying no
to," I lament to Mrs. Brandt. But apparently the boys do know.
The superhero cannot bear to be unmasked and found want-
ing; he likes to play what he has already played.

The girls have been "playing school" all year. They bring
crayons, pencils, and papers into the doll corner, and "lessons"
are imposed in a highly structured manner.

> Charlotte: Everyone say "Two and two is four."
> Girls: Two and two is four.
> Charlotte: Write down "Two and two is four."
> Karen: I can't make a two.
> Charlotte: You're a bad girl. You didn't do your
>   homework.
> Karen: Okay, teacher. Next time I will.

My lessons are as legitimate as Charlotte's, for the girls. If I,
for example, lay out multicolored paper strips and demonstrate
how to weave them into checkerboard mats, the girls will continue to make mats long after the lesson is over. For them it is
play. The boys stay away and reinforce the notion that they
don't like it and won't do well.

Even Franklin is distrustful when the assignment is set by the teacher. To please the boys, I organize projects based on outer space and racing cars, but the response is only momentarily enthusiastic. It is not play if the teacher presides, and if it is not play, then it could be a cause for worry.

What difference does it make if the girls choose to "play" with the teacher and the boys prefer to copy one another? In both instances their skills are improving. Nonetheless, the habit of excluding school from play has repercussions for many boys, who begin to think they are not good at schoolwork.

The value of playing school is that you cannot fail. Those who play a great deal at table tasks may take the feeling with them when the real thing comes along. Perhaps it is not practice but *pretend* practice that makes perfect. Of course, when the boys copy Franklin's pictures, they are playing school and don't know it. They have seen themselves on the outside for so long they don't recognize when the Rubicon has been crossed.

I often watch the nursery school children next door "at work." The youngest boys and girls start at about the same place; that is, they are equally unskilled. Delighted by the novelty of messy, colorful art materials, they draw, tear paper, and smear paste without regard for the finished product. It seems splendid enough that crayons make marks on paper, that paper can be torn or cut, and that paste makes paper slippery. The paints drip and flow and change colors in magical ways. The children are not making "something"; they are simply making.

The boys, however, quickly become discouraged. The novelty is soon over and they want speedier improvements. Others around them are drawing real pictures while they cannot seem to make the crayons respond properly. In any case, these table activities require too much sitting; they know they would be better off playing with cars. Once inside the block area, they find cars, trucks, and older boys much more to their liking. And so they switch from "schoolwork" back to floor play. The teacher does not have to label one "work" and one "play"; since teachers are usually at the tables, that must be "work."

While the boys are deciding that table work is too hard and takes too long, the three-year-old girls have already made it a habit. The tables offer a safe haven as they become accustomed to so many noisy, pushy boys. The teacher is there, the older girls are making things, and it is almost like being in the kitchen with mother.

There are other reasons why the girls do not associate table work with feelings of impatience and frustration. Their skills are improving at a faster rate; they are beginning to draw identifiable pictures when most of the boys still cannot make two lines meet. The only boys who remain at the tables after the initial exploratory period are the few whose coordination is exceptional and who receive instant gratification. For the rest, the rewards do not come quickly enough. Boys want things to happen fast. They leave the table for the best of reasons: They are not ready. Unfortunately, the boys think they have left because they are superheroes, and they spend the next two years defending that position.

By the time boys enter kindergarten, there seems to be an inverse connection between superhero play and table work, whereas the real connection is between table play and table work. The boys, in fact, are ready to pick up where they left off at age three; they are ready to play school.

One thing that is needed, perhaps, is for the lesson plans to be put away for a while so the boys can finally realize it is play after all.

33

I have crossed an important threshold. Children's play has become more real to me than my own ideas of "work." Eager to see how one kind of play leads to another, I have doubled the time spent in free play: Morning playtime is now ninety minutes and the afternoon session one hour. Surprisingly, the girls spend the extra time in the doll corner and the blocks, while the boys go to the tables.

Earlier in the year, the boys used most of each play period for block play. Cleanup time invariably caught them unprepared. "We didn't get a chance to play yet!" "It took us the whole time to build. We didn't play in it!"

With the expanded schedule, the total time spent in spaceships and hideouts remains the same but is spread out over a longer period. The pace is less frantic; the block area is home base rather than walled fortress. In between Star Wars episodes the boys give equal time to other activities, including the arts and crafts they slighted before.

Is it the longer playtimes or the decrease in direct instruction that makes table activities more desirable? In this class both conditions seem necessary. No matter how long the boys play, they do not choose my checkerboard mats and number charts, whereas ambiguous materials left on the tables attract and hold them. A checkerboard mat means precise expectations, and it is these expectations that make the boys uncomfortable. There is no way to prove it, but I think their drawing and printing skills have flourished under the minimal attention paid them this year.

There is a renaissance of table activities. The boys draw a new kind of racing car with fancy stripes and three-digit numerals, and they have tic-tac-toe tournaments that are noisier and more competitive than Star Wars. Mindful that first grade is approaching, I bring back my lesson plans, carefully scheduling work between the two play periods. The boys seem satisfied with the arrangement.

More observations: As long as we have two long playtimes, fantasy play occupies less than half of each period. However, if for some reason the morning session is curtailed or eliminated, the boys resort to old habits and segregate themselves in the block area during the afternoon. The girls make up the lost time at the art tables. They say, "We haven't made anything yet!" The boys say, "We didn't play yet!"

I have come to an unavoidable conclusion: My curriculum has suited girls better than boys. For too long my cue has come from the girls, who play at the tables with or without the teacher. The maxim that play is the work of the young child is valid when children define their own play. Furthermore, if Jack is allowed to climb the beanstalk first, there is a better chance he will seek out work the moment he comes down.

34 Television does not invent the way boys play, but it fits the mode comfortably. Even our doubled play periods are not long enough to respond to everything seen on the TV screen.

During a two-day period in May the boys tell eleven stories: three Star Wars, two Mighty Mouses, one Superman, one jailhouse, two Draculas, one Woody Woodpecker, and one Tom and Jerry. Except for Star Wars, the inspiration for all the stories comes from television. (The girls dictated eight stories on those two days and did not include a single television or movie character.)

1. Once there was Woody Woodpecker. He was making a house. This lady was a bird watcher and she saw Woody Woodpecker and she was trying to get him. He said, "Look—there's a bird. Get on it." So the lady got on the bird and the bird ate her up. She was dead. The bird tried to eat Woody Woodpecker, but it couldn't.

2. One day Wolfman was guarding the door of the castle. Then a fake Frankenstein knocked at the door, but the real Frankenstein knew it was just a man, so he told Dracula. So Dracula sucked out all his blood. He died.

3. There was a big creaky house. Whoever walked by it gets killed, and they turn into monsters. And one time Dracula was having a fight with the president. And Wolfman got killed and turned into the Wolfman mummy. He killed twenty people that walked by the

house. That makes twenty monsters. Then there was no people left, only monsters.

4. Once there was two men. One was white and one was black. They took a shower. The police came and said, "Who are you, good guys or bad guys?" They said, "We're bad guys." They didn't know they were talking to police. The two men were put in jail. But they climbed out. One took out a knife and the other took out a gun. They killed the police.

5. Once upon a time there was Superman and Superdog. Then Wonderwoman came and told Superman there was a monster. Then they went inside their Superman house. Then Superman killed the monster.

6. Once upon a time there was a store and it had mice in it. One day some cats came and sneaked up on them. The mice ran. Some of them got eaten. Then Mighty Mouse came and punched the cat and then he killed him with his power.

7. One time a cat was chasing a mouse, and Mighty Mouse came. Then he punched the cat. Then he killed the cat. He let the mice go from where the cat put them inside the boxes. Then another cat came and then Mighty Mouse killed the cat, but he was too weak to kill the cat, so the cat killed Mighty Mouse.

8. Once upon a time Luke and Han Solo were looking for Count Dracula. He called to Wolfman. He came to Count Dracula. Count Dracula called his workmen, but Luke shot one of the workmen. Count Dracula closed up the castle. Luke and Han Solo broke in. Then Count Dracula sucked their blood out and put them in jail.

9. Once upon a time there was Darth Vader and two storm troopers talking to Han Solo. Darth

said, "Why are you killing me?" Han said, "You're just a robot." Luke cut off the storm troopers' heads. But Darth called IG-2 and told them to get Luke. So Luke and Han said, "Hurry. Let's go to Cloud City."

10. Once Tom was looking for Jerry. Then Jerry was running from Tom. They went to a spooky house and there was Count Dracula. He was disguised to be a witch, so he had a broom. "Get on my broom." But they knew who it was, so they killed him and kept the broom.

11. Once upon a time Luke lived in his hideout. Then he got out of his hideout and so did Darth Vader. They had a sword fight. While they were having a sword fight, Han Solo and Chewbacca were shooting in their *Millennium Falcon* at the storm troopers. That time nobody won the war. It was a tie.

The impact of television on boys can be seen by anyone who watches them play; however, its effect on school behavior is difficult to assess. I am certain that superhero play begins at an earlier age than it did thirty years ago, and that the boys leave the doll corner at least a year ahead of schedule. Certainly there is a wider variety of violence pictured today in stories and play, but not more actual fighting. The increase in mock-aggressive fantasy play may even lessen the need for real combat.

I watched thirty minutes of Spiderman one day in the block area. Six boys built and destroyed two hideouts, shot and trapped one another in webs and trash compactors, made one jail for storm troopers and then another for good guys, and fashioned a sizeable collection of weapons. There were only two angry encounters, both over the possession of the same toy.

On this particular occasion, Teddy was Batman. He likes superhero play now, but only in the classroom. Teddy wants rules and order. He wants to stop when he's had enough, and this is more easily achieved indoors. Teddy has become my radar signal. If he joins a superhero exercise, I can turn my back and become involved elsewhere. He will not long remain in a situation that threatens to get out of hand; if the boys want him to stay, they know they must play in a calmer manner.

The girls serve the same purpose. Supergirl and Wonderwoman have a modifying effect on any group of boys. They are always made welcome and usually emphasize the living arrangements in the block area. When Charlotte is Wonderwoman, dinner is served right inside the spaceship, and Darth Vader behaves suspiciously like father coming home from work.

35

The boys and girls watch one another closely and are aware of any new interest on either side of the circle.

Andrew: All the girls love Strawberry Shortcake now.

Teacher: I wonder why that is.

Andrew: They think she has a nice smell.

Teacher: Do you like that smell?

Andrew: Boys don't like smells.

Teacher: Don't like smells?

Andrew: I mean boys like bad smells. I mean dangerous smells. Like volcano smells.

Jonathan: Vampire smells.

Teacher: Well, Strawberry Shortcake doesn't have to worry about volcanoes or vampires. The girls never put those things in their stories.

Teddy: Because vampires aren't pretty. We like stuff that isn't pretty, but not girls. They like only pretty things.

The boys are talking about a new doll called Strawberry Shortcake. Her sudden appearance in such large numbers may, of course, reflect an extensive advertising campaign, but is surely owing in part to the relief felt by mothers at the sight of a doll that looks like a little girl and smells like a lollipop.

Each doll has a scent and dress color that match its name: Strawberry Shortcake, Raspberry Tart, Orange Blossom, and so on. They are self-contained odes to uncomplicated visions, inspiring dozens of stories about friends going to parties.

> One day there was a princess named Strawberry Shortcake and she had two babies called Apple and Apricot. She told her friend Raspberry Tart, and Raspberry bought them a bunny and a turtle and they had a birthday party. (Mary Ann)

> Once upon a time there was a little girl named Strawberry Shortcake. Raspberry said to Strawberry, "Where are you going?" Strawberry said, "To a tea party." Raspberry said, "Can I come with you?" Strawberry said, "Yes." So they went and they met Huckleberry Pie, Apricot and Bunny, Apple Dumpling, Orange Blossom, Lemon Meringue, and Blueberry Muffin. (Charlotte)

Magical characters and innovative plots are not required, because nothing disturbing will take place. The announcement of a new Strawberry Shortcake story brings a smile to every girl's face, and to a few boys' as well.

The flurry of Strawberry Shortcake stories highlights the absence of stories about Barbie dolls. Though the girls bring their Barbie dolls to school frequently now, they seem unsure of her image.

They put all the other dolls into their stories, but not Barbie. When Mary Ann brings her Snow White doll, there are half a dozen Snow White stories that same day. Janie's Pocahontas doll inspires Indian-princess stories for a week. Mysteriously, Barbie is left out. Or rather Barbie is left out because she is a mystery, to be dressed and combed but not explored too openly.

Much that girls experience intensely in the doll corner does not enter into their stories. Taboos in play are few, but a five-year-old girl wants story material that is free of worry or can be easily disguised. The nursery school girl says straight out,

"Once upon a time a father moved out of my house and took his radio." In kindergarten she may insert the actual events into doll-corner play, but she conceals and enlarges them when she dictates a story: "The king found a new palace, and the princess lived with him and made him a prince." Fairy tales are a boon to girl storytellers.

Boys seldom need such stratagems, since their play has already masked sensitive issues. Storytelling for them is primarily a recall of superhero themes. When something makes a boy sad, he simply becomes a more powerful superhero. He is not compelled to act out confusing events face to face, as are the girls.

Why is Barbie in this sensitive category of family secrets? Visually she is not so different from the Cinderella doll; both are nubile maidens, lavishly clothed, and held in high esteem by all the girls. However, Cinderella is protected by magic and receives adult approval; Barbie is given uncertain acceptance. Any character named Cinderella is a safe stand-in for the storyteller when troublesome ideas are aired. Cinderella can lose a mother, gain a new father, or live alone in the woods. She can afford to be excessively happy or sad, because magical forces will come to her aid. Barbie, like Goldilocks, has no fairy godmother and is alone in the woods. And besides, the girls sense that there are aspects of Barbie that ought not be talked about openly.

> Teacher: How do you play house with a Barbie doll?
> Charlotte: We pretend they are the sister and the mommy.
> Teacher: Then who are you?
> Janie: We're the one that acts them out.
> Teacher: Oh. You *are* the Barbie doll.
> Janie: Right. We *are* the sister or mommy.
> Teacher: But you're the sister and mommy even without Barbie.
> Jill: This is much more funner. Because you can look at her and see how she looks.
> Teacher: By the way, how old is she supposed to be?

The girls blush and giggle as if I have asked an indelicate question. I have never seen them so ill at ease in a discussion.

> Charlotte: Maybe a teenager.
> Teacher: But sometimes she's a mother?
> Charlotte: No.
> Janie: Yes. Uh . . . I don't know. Yes, she is.
> Teacher: Do you ever pretend she's a mother with a baby?
> Charlotte: No! No! She never has a baby. Never!
> Jill: Of course not. No babies.
> Janie: But we pretend to have babies. Right, Mary Ann? Remember?

There are more side glances and embarrassed laughter; Barbie is not open to full analysis. By contrast, nothing is covert about superhero dolls.

> Teacher: How old is Han Solo?
> Andrew: About twenty seven or seventeen.
> Teddy: Maybe he's thirty four. My daddy is thirty four.
> Franklin: Uh-uh. He ain't a father yet. He's a brother.
> Teacher: Is he old enough to get married?
> Jonathan: Yeah, he could. He could marry Princess Leia.
> Andrew: He can't. She's his boss.
> Teacher: How about Batman? Is he a father?
> All the boys: He's Robin's father.
> Teacher: Who is the mother?
> Teddy: Wonderwoman.
> Franklin: No she ain't, Teddy. They don't tell you that.

All my questions are taken as legitimate. Superheroes, as is true of Cinderella or Snow White, are in the public domain. All information can be—and should be—pursued. The Barbie doll exists in another context. She is not associated with a fairy tale, nor is she comfortably included in the family, yet she is a woman who looks more like mother than any other doll, and the girls unabashedly love her.

I make an impromptu visit to the kindergarten down the hall: Every girl says Barbie is her favorite, most imply that their mothers disapprove, and the teachers tell me privately they wish Barbie dolls were left at home.

36 Feminine splurges are often followed by a closer look at what the boys are doing.

Charlotte: The boys never put girls in their stories.
  Then they get all the turns when it's their stories
  to act.
Andrew: Princess Leia we do.
Charlotte: You always pick Mary Ann. Only her.
Teacher: You girls don't want to take the other parts.
Charlotte: All right. I will. I'll be Luke. Or a storm
  trooper. A monster!
Teacher: Paul's story is next. There's a part for
  Frankenstein and Dracula and four soldiers.
Paul: They could be the soldiers, Me and Andrew are
  Dracula and Frankenstein.

Charlotte and Janie stand in the middle of the circle, motionless soldiers, while four boys run about shooting and yelling. When the narrative is over, Charlotte says, "See, I *told* you I would be a soldier!" The boys are uncritical of the girls' lackluster performances; they do not expect girls to behave as boys do.

Charlotte, the great adaptor, now figures out a way to bring Andrew into her story. The offending line "When the prince saw she was prettier than a rose he could not help to kiss her" is changed to ". . . he could not help to look at her."

"Andrew, do you want to be the prince?"

"What does he do?"

"Nothing. He looks at me. No kissing."

"Okay."

Andrew enters the stage on a horse and gallops around the circle for the duration of the story. No horse is called for in the script, but Charlotte is content. Kissing and marriage are temporarily dispensed with in exchange for a real boy prince.

The boys are not so accommodating. They admit girls into their stories, but will not alter the prose.

"Can't you make it a friendly monster?" Mary Ann asks Andrew after hearing his latest story. "If you do, I'll be the monster."

"No. Real monsters are not friendly."

Andrew's response seems proper. A boy does not spend three years scaring people only to then casually drop the pose. Girls may rechannel kissing if they wish, but the integrity of Andrew's monster is inviolable, or so he would like to think. Actually, a crack in the armor is beginning to appear.

"What if we only pretend to rob you?" Andrew asks several girls in the doll corner one day.

Charlotte gives him a long look. "What do you mean?"

"Pretend we're not really robbers, and we come in very quietly and you're asleep."

Mary Ann picks up the idea. "Pretend we're the sleeping princesses and you're the dwarfs and you pretend to be robbers."

"Pretend we live in a castle," Jonathan says excitedly, "and we need your jewels for the buried treasure——"

"No," interrupts Charlotte. "You're the dwarfs and you live in a cave and you sneak in and we're asleep and then the dog barks and we wake up——"

"Pretend we're pretend dwarfs and we're really robbers but you think we're dwarfs," Andrew urges.

"Pretend you're a prince but you look like a dwarf and pretend you're not really a robber——"

"I don't want to be a prince."

"A dwarf?"

"Okay. A dwarf," Andrew agrees.

"And a pretend robber," Mary Ann adds.

"Okay. Pretend."

This seems to be an admirably innovative approach to the ongoing doll-corner robber problem. There have been regular break-ins to the doll corner since we debated the matter, including a spate of robberies while the girls were in room 214.

"Pretend we're pretend robbers" might solve that touchy doll-corner dilemma over the acceptability of robbers in female territory. The idea of dwarfs masquerading as robbers is a coup de theatre for the girls.

The boys begin to build the dwarfs' cave, then hurriedly add on a castle "for the buried dynamite." Dynamite? At the mention of the word, a magical reversal takes place. Andrew runs to the junk basket for an armful of toilet-paper tubes, which he and Jonathan tie together in small bundles. Meanwhile Teddy, Paul, and Robert extend the castle until it overlooks the doll corner.

Unaware of any script changes, the girls hide the jewels and prepare an elaborate bedding arrangement that utilizes every shelf and chair. Suddenly the doll corner is bombarded with sticks of dynamite and loud explosions. The pretend robbers swoop down on the jewels, hidden under the doll-corner table, and race back to the castle.

Instantly the girls are at my side. "They're doing it again! They're spoiling everything!"

"I'm surprised the plan didn't work out better," I say, on the way to the castle.

"We're playing castle," Andrew says. "See, I was on the tower and I was——pretending to throw dynamite and——"

"You didn't pretend! It was real," Charlotte says.

"Real?" I ask.

"I mean real pretend. I mean he really threw it."

"I wasn't really throwing. I was pretending. See, I reached over and it dropped out of my hand."

"Andrew, what happened to the dwarfs sneaking in quietly?" I ask.

"See, the dwarfs found dynamite under the castle where the robbers buried it there."

The boys and girls look at one another without rancor. Robbers, after all, are bad guys, and princesses are required to protest. But I, the teacher, am not a princess and need not act as if the superheroes will pull down the classroom walls.

Let the boys be robbers, then, or tough guys in space. It is the natural, universal, and essential play of little boys. Everything is make-believe except the obvious feelings of well-being that emerge from fantasy play.

Can the superhero controversy yield to so simple a solution? Have I come to like the characters and the plot more than I admire a quiet room?